Praise for *101 Secrets for*

Like advice from a wiser, funnier, older br[...] done that, and wants to save you some pain
> —SETH GODIN, *New York Times* bestseller and author of
> *The Icarus Deception*

You can be frustrated, fearful, and stressed out about your twenties, or you can read this book, get a wake-up call, and put yourself on the right path. Paul's advice on how to be successful in your twenties is timely, important, and will help you feel more confident in your own skin.
> —DAN SCHAWBEL, bestselling author of *Me 2.0* and
> *Promote Yourself*

Life will never feel like it's supposed to. That's just one of the many motivating gems in Paul Angone's *101 Secrets for Your Twenties*, which is the mid-to-late millennials' answer to the quarterlife crisis. As a companion to Paul's successful website, AllGroanUp.com, the book gets to the heart of the worries on every twentysomething's mind and addresses them with straight-talk and humor.
> —ALEXANDRA LEVIT, author of *Blind Spots: The 10 Business*
> *Myths You Can't Afford to Believe on Your New Path to*
> *Success*

This book is funny, heartfelt, and important. Your twenties are a time of life that most people tend to glamorize or dismiss. Paul does neither. I especially liked #6.
> —JEFF GOINS, author of *Wrecked: When a Broken World*
> *Slams into Your Comfortable Life*

I love this book. *101 Secrets for Your Twenties* is like a concentrated blender-shot of fluorescent green, ice crystally advice, insight, and wisdom. Toss your head back and enjoy the cold jolt.
> —NEIL PASRICHA, author of the *New York Times* bestseller
> *The Book of Awesome*

101 Secrets is a masterpiece. Full of brilliant advice wrapped in belly-laughing hilarity, Paul Angone has a true gift for troubleshooting the trials and tribulations of post-grad adulthood. This book is a must-read for twentysomethings and beyond who are struggling with how to navigate in today's hyper-connected, chaotic world—and the book itself is formatted as a fun, engaging page-turner. Paul promises "wheelbarrows full of wisdom-stuffed pearls, laced with humor and vulnerability," and that's exactly what you're going to get. Just don't ask him to whip you up a Venti half-caff 2.5-shot sugar-free-vanilla no-foam upside-down latte.

—JENNY BLAKE, author of *Life After College: The Complete Guide to Getting What You Want*

Paul gives humorously wise insights that will give twentysomethings a sneak peek of what's to come, perspective that will help them breathe, and the reality that they aren't alone. My top three . . . er . . . sixteen were: #2, #3, #7, #9, #18, #21, #24, #38, #47, #77, #80, #84, #87, #95, #100 and #10's nineteenth sign made me say, "TRUTH!" out loud. Being the ripe 30-year-old that I am, you can trust me.

—JOY EGGERICHS, director of Love and Respect Now

Paul is an emerging voice for this generation. He understands the unique struggle of those going through the rocky, ambiguous, thrilling decade of their twenties and has a gift for delivering rock solid truth packaged in laugh out loud humor.

—CHRISTINE HASSLER, author of *20 Something Manifesto*, speaker, life coach

101 Secrets is the perfect mix of humor and wisdom. I read it in a single sitting, but the insights will stick with me for a long time. My favorites are #2, #5, #33, #71, #81, and #97 (plus several more but I was only allowed to pick a few). Where was this book when I graduated from college?

—ALLISON VESTERFELT, author of *Packing Light*

What Paul Angone has done in *101 Secrets for Your Twenties* may well be the definitive field manual for post-graduates. He's a gifted writer, blending humor, stories, truth, and advice in a way that makes anyone the wiser for picking this up. Best of all, he helps young people lay a foundation for success later in life. If you don't believe me, then read #7, #19, or #61.

—SAM DAVIDSON, author, college speaker, social entrepreneur

I always tell people that I'm enjoying my 30s way more than my 20s and now I know why: I didn't have this book! Secrets #21 and #36 alone would have helped me through so many situations. I can't tell you how

happy I am that this book exists for the next generation!
—BRYAN ALLAIN, author of *This is NOT a Treasure Map*
and *Actually, Clams Are Miserable*

As a recent escapee of my twenties, I wish I had been given a book like this when I graduated from college. In an age when we are led to believe that a college diploma is a winning lottery ticket for a dream job, and uber-success is as easy as writing the perfect status update on Facebook, Paul's book is a fantastic, fun, and above all *true* guide for the often frustrated, fearful, or just flat broke twentysomething. Keep a special lookout for secrets #8, #21, and #76. Secret #76 has been pretty much the last ten years for me.
—MATT APPLING, teacher, pastor and author of *Life after Art: What You Forgot About Life and Faith Since You Left the Art Room*

101 Secrets for Your Twenties is a refreshingly honest compilation of life truths. Paul Angone has cleverly put into words our twentysomething experience, yet with a passionate and purposeful goal of helping young adults navigate this unique stage in life without regret. If you're like me, you'll laugh (especially at secrets #5, #17, and #44), ponder (secrets #29 and #43), and say a lot of "Amens!" along the way (secrets #1, #21, and #53).
—ADAM YORK, editor, *Collegiate* magazine

Paul knows twentysomethings. He shares secrets that are really gold, even to non-twentysomethings. Gold to understanding twentysomethings. Gold to understanding today. Understanding this generation. Understanding your kids. The book helps me be a better father . . . a better pastor. I feel more prepared. Don't tell my boys . . . or the young people at my church. It's supposed to be a secret.
—RON EDMONDSON, pastor, organizational leadership consultant

A subtitle for this book might well be "How do you face the realities of life in your twenties?" Paul treats the issues one faces whether they are career-related, personal relationships, or individual hang-ups in addition to a host of other issues with amazing honesty, creativity, and wisdom beyond his years. I wish his *101 Secrets* had been in print when I was entering my late and post-teen years. Whether it be secret #7, #27, or #77, or any of his 101 secrets, Paul provides incredible insight in helping a young person cope with a wide variety of life issues. This is a great read at any age, but especially valuable for young adults and I highly recommend it!

—DAVID C. BICKER, PhD, Professor Emeritus and Founding Chair of the Department of Communication Studies at Azusa Pacific University

Introducing Paul Angone. A raw human being. A fellow human struggler. A creative, gifted writer who is good at making fun of himself. Paul sort of splats out his frustrations in delineated fashion and then tidies them up into a comedy act and finalizes the show with some serious good advice that applies to people well beyond their twenties. If you're looking for your destiny and can't find it, then steal away somewhere and read this book. It's a punchy, non-preachy pep talk that will help you persevere and not settle for something less like mediocrity.

—SARAH SUMNER, author of *Men and Women in the Church*

This is the kind of book that I wish I had read when I was in my twenties. It would have saved me from some unnecessary trial-and-error experiences including the anxiety that came with some of my ill-informed choices. Paul's humorous approach to some of life's early challenges will help the reader maintain a healthy perspective as some common assumptions are challenged. My favorite secret is #62, which I believe to be the key to life-long healthy living.

—RAY ROOD, founder of The Genysys Group

When I read Paul Angone's second secret, I was hooked: "The possibility for greatness and embarrassment both exist in the same space. If you're not willing to be embarrassed, you're probably not willing to be great." Paul's capacity for embarrassment makes his book a very, very funny book. It's worth reading if for no other reason that it will make you laugh out loud as it did me. But it is much more: it is wise. I've worked with so-called twentysomethings for twenty years, and I have stopped reading the boring dissertations social scientists write to explain these folks. Paul's collection of zany epigrams beats them all, hands down.

—BEN PATTERSON, campus pastor, Westmont College

101
Secrets
For Your
Twenties

PAUL ANGONE

MOODY PUBLISHERS
CHICAGO

Cover spread design: Tan Nguyen
Cover image design: Natalie Mills
Interior design: Erik Peterson

Secret #87 originally published on LoveandRespectNow.com
Secrets #38 and #96 originally published on RELEVANTMagazine.com

Library of Congress Cataloging-in-Publication Data

Angone, Paul.
    101 secrets for your twenties / Paul Angone.
      pages cm
    ISBN 978-0-8024-1084-9
    1. Young adults—United States—Life skills guides. 2. Success. I. Title.
  II. Title: One hundred one secrets for your twenties. III. Title: One hundred
  and one secrets for your twenties.
  HQ799.7.A54 2013
  305.242—dc23

We hope you enjoy this book from Moody Publishers. Our goal is to provide high-quality, thought-provoking books and products that connect truth to your real needs and challenges. For more information on other books and products written and produced from a biblical perspective, go to www.moodypublishers.com or write to:

Moody Publishers
820 N. La Salle Boulevard
Chicago, IL 60610

7 9 10 8

Printed in the United States of America

To my wife Naomi—I love you and would need a whole book in itself to properly thank you.

To my daughters Hannalise and Sierrah—you are unbelievably amazing. Twenty years from now, I hope this book will encourage you.

Contents

Introduction

LIGHTS . . . CAMERA . . .

Cue a 26-year-old male. Brown hair. Parted to the left. A face that both mothers and daughters can agree on. Getting ready for his job selling advertising space for a midsized website.

Let's call him Peter.

Peter grabs a light blue dress shirt, snapping it in the air a few times like he's trying to knock out a salmon. Hoping the violent motion will somehow shake the wrinkles.

He doesn't remember exactly when he stopped ironing his dress shirts before work. It wasn't a conscious decision. He just grabbed the iron one morning, stared at it for a few moments, and put it back in the closet.

In the grand scheme of things, wrinkles just didn't seem worth the time.

An A- student in college. The editor in chief of the university newspaper. Peter had big plans as he crossed the graduation stage—to be a journalist, maybe an editor, at the city newspaper. His dream was to write stories that matter. To highlight the good going on in the world instead of the bad.

Everyone knew Peter would make it.

Through a friend's dad he was able to land an internship. Worked hard. Started getting a few small assignments. Could see some light at the beginning of his dream. Landed his first big interview with the mayor.

Then, his whole department was laid off.

Cue scrambling to find a job anywhere. Cue selling advertising space. Cue vague memories of the last two years, each day blending together in a kaleidoscope of monotony.

Peter can't really complain about his job. Oh, he used too. Every day. But not now. He's settled in. Good wage. Good hours. Good boss. Good corner-cubicle and if he leans backward far enough and to the left, he can just see the window and the top branches of an elm tree.

His dreams of being a journalist have slowly died. But his 401(k) is alive and well.

THE LOOMING QUESTION

But as he loops his tie this morning and cinches the knot, his hands move to a standstill. He stares into the mirror, his eyes locking like two spies trying to tell if the other is lying or telling the truth.

Then THE QUESTION hits him. One that he's been avoiding. He wants to run from it even now, but it's caught him like a shrimp in a net.

What am I doing with my life?

There. He's said it.

He has a good wage at a good job. Monotonous, meaningless, mundane . . .

But my life was supposed to matter. To have an impact. To do something worth doing.

Our generation's greatest question has gripped him tight this morning and is not letting go.

WHAT NOW?

Peter's story is my story. And maybe it's yours too. Sure the details are different, but I believe **What Now?** is the question looming in the back of our generation's closet.

There is a collective **Twentysomething-Struggle** going on. We're being propelled into the rest of our lives and nothing can bring us back. How do we make sure we're shot in the right direction, while not being splattered across any windshields in the process?

MY STORY

For years in my 20s I experienced ample amounts of my own *un-success*. I became bitter. Frustrated. Angry at God, man, and myself. My 20s weren't turning out to be the successfest I'd planned and somebody, *everybody* was to blame.

What was I doing wrong? Why were all my big dreams and plans mere fairy tales to life's blunt reality? Was everyone else sailing on the **Rock Your 20s Cruise Ship** and somehow I'd missed that boat?

Sitting on a not-so-glamorous motel room floor, while traveling for my less-than-ideal sales job, I made a pact with myself, God, and that '80s floral motel bedspread right next to me: **I was going to find the secrets to doing my 20s right.** Because up to that point it all felt nothing but wrong.

Little did I know this search for these twentysomething-secrets would take the rest of my 20s to discover.

DECADE-LONG SEARCH

My search for the secrets journeyed through a master's program, a slew of lousy jobs, reading books galore, thousands of conversations, interviewing business leaders, interviewing twentysomethings who were actually experiencing success, and even interviewing elderly people in retirement homes with the hopes of living in one to glean from people at the end of their story to speak into our beginning.

My search went near and far and back again.

Finally, one Sunday afternoon I decided to write an article called *21 Secrets for Your 20s* on my website AllGroanUp.com—my initial stab at formulating what I felt were the true, funny, encouraging, challenging, and honest secrets that I'd set out to find years ago.

Three days after posting that article, my website crashed due to tsunami waves of traffic.

I didn't know such a thing was possible.

I called my web host. Pleaded with them to turn my site back on.

Two days later, my website crashed again and lay shipwrecked on an island in the Philippines for five hours.

I didn't know such a thing was possible.

Literally thousands of emails from twentysomethings began pouring into my inbox. A senior in college from Indonesia, a 24-year-old gal from Kenya, a recent grad from Wyoming, a professional in New York. Twentysomethings from all over the globe, in all settings with all backgrounds, were communicating to me their gratitude and the relief they felt knowing they were not alone in the trials and experiences unique to this decade. We were all going through the same stuff.

These 21 secrets were speaking into a collective story and struggle, and yet, I knew there were many more secrets that needed to be shared.

CUE: 101 SECRETS FOR YOUR 20s

I think we can all agree: This twentysomething shoot ain't easy. It's a decade exploding with intensity and ambiguity. Anxiety and excitement. Purpose and pointlessness. Answers riddled with questions. Paradoxes mixed with 100 percent certainties. There are so many "firsts." So much change. So many *what ifs, what nows, and what the hecks.*

So for that reason, I'm not going to get all rosy, chipper "change the world" on you in this book like a graduation speaker hyped up on coffee and their speaking fee.

But I'm also not going to be all grim, dire, and serious like the weight of the world is on each page.

What I promise is wheelbarrows full of wisdom-stuffed pearls, laced with humor and vulnerability. I'd love to leave the vulnerability wheelbarrow hidden in the garage and come off as one of those uber-successful, don't-you-wish-you-were-me authors. But I don't see how I can share "secrets" without turning the lock and opening up the black box. Without vulnerability, this book would be titled *101 Partial Truths and Platitudes for Your 20s.* And that's not exactly life-changing material.

HERE WE GO

This book is for every Peter, Paul, and Penelope wrestling with "what now?"

2,555 days ago when I began looking for the truth to our 20s, I didn't realize that it would take being body slammed by massive questions, studying, searching, pleading, pushing, crying, caffeinating, praying, failing, and failing, and failing, wondering if I'd lost my mind, researching, experiencing mild success sandwiched in-between modest failure, crying to God to be transported to my 30s, being lost and then found time and time again to reach this point.

These secrets that I'm about to share with you were not easily obtained. All I ask is that you do something with them. Or even better, allow the possibility of them doing something with you.

Sometimes surviving your 20s is nothing more glamorous than just holding on for dear life on the back of an inner tube like a kid being whipped around by a speedboat.

You can't see a thing.

Repeated waves knock the wind out of you.

Your hands are gripped so tight your fingers begin to cramp.

And your only choice of survival is to **just let go.**

2

The possibility for greatness and embarrassment both exist in the same space. If you're not willing to be embarrassed, you're probably not willing to be great.

A couple years ago while riding my bike at a park, I came across a peculiar, once-in-a-lifetime sight—a Beach Boys cover band up on a stage playing to a crowd of about 500 people. Like a moth to the flame of '60s music I stood there, when the band made an announcement:

"For our last song we need five volunteers to come on stage and play some air guitar. The crowd will vote on the best performance with the winner getting this!" The lead singer held up a beautiful, white Les Paul guitar. "First five that make it up front, make it on stage!"

Free guitar!? I couldn't have pulled up at a better time as I had a 50-foot head start on anyone in the crowd. People began to stand. A few started to run. I took two steps. Then froze. I looked at the size of the crowd. Anxiety rushed through me like I'd downed three Mountain Dews before running with the bulls.

Making a fool of myself for a free guitar? Was it worth it?

I didn't know a soul in the crowd. Get me on stage and I'll come alive and put on a show. But that takes me *actually* getting on stage.

I deliberated. I debated. And by the time I slowly sauntered over, they had chosen the five.

I missed the moment.

I then watched the five who made it on stage give halfhearted, lame attempts at air guitar that would've made Jimi Hendrix cry—their fear of embarrassment making it embarrassing. I felt sick because that guitar could've been mine.

But you have to be on the stage to win. They weren't going to give the guitar to the bystander in the front row who swore he could've done it better.

THE FEAR OF EMBARRASSMENT KILLS

The possibility for embarrassment and greatness usually exist in the same space. It's difficult to remove one and not the other. When you do, you exist in the middle. Mediocrity your brand. No one saying a thing about you—good or bad. Why would they?

That's where I've existed most days. How many moments have I lived in a sterile, white-walled existence where my *perceived appearance* is the wild card that trumps all?

Well nuts to that. Let's overnight the fear of embarrassment to the unreachable depths of the south pole.

The fear of embarrassment poisons creativity.

The fear of embarrassment stifles risk.

The fear of embarrassment lets insecurities call the shots.

Embarrassment thrives like a fungus in the petri dish of *"what will others think?"*

Who cares what others think?

Let them exist in the middle.

I want my guitar.

Who's with me?

Making and keeping friendships in your 20s is harder than G.I. Joe's abs.

Making friends was so easy when we were kids. Or at least that's how my nostalgia remembers it.

You tackled a kid at recess. Partnered with someone for Bio Lab. Played a basketball game at the park. Got cast in a play. Moved into a dorm.

Then *bam*, you had a friend.

Lots of them.

Like the kid whose dad worked for Nintendo—friends just waiting at your doorstep.

And then college happened—the height of *Friend Mania.*

And then college ended and with it, so did many of your friendships.

WHERE DID ALL THE FRIENDSHIPS GO????

Then you entered the abyss—the *Friend Abyss.*

Your 20s and 30s are deep, uncharted waters where friends are dumped in black bags never to be seen again.

All those *friends-are-friends-forever* friends, gone—the apparent expiration date on "forever" lasting about two and a half years.

Because you move. Get married. Have kids. Or work a 60-hour a week job. Keeping friendships in your 20s becomes harder than G.I. Joe's abs (*that's prison-walls-hard, people*) because you don't have the same shared experiences anymore. You're not going to class, then eating lunch, going to practice, eating dinner, hanging out until 2 a.m. like you did in college.

Now your best friend calls and the first thought in your head might be, "Really. *Now.* I don't have time."

You stare at the phone as if to say "I'm sorry" as the ring lets out one last cry for help before it's sent to voicemail like a kid sent to detention for not showing up on time.

Maybe you'll call back in a day, or maybe a week. But most likely when you do, you'll get voicemail too. Then you'll begin the respected twentysomething tradition: **Voicemail Tag**. Almost as fun as freeze tag when we were kids, with one big difference—it's not fun at all.

So after a couple back-and-forths on voicemail, then a couple texts, then a couple Facebook messages—next thing you know your *friendship* has been reduced to throwing out the once-a-year "*Happy B-Day!!!!*" Facebook wall post, giving it four "!!!!" to show just how excited you really are about your friend (check that friendship off for another year).

MAKING NEW FRIENDS

If keeping up with old friends is *hard*, making new ones is *Bruce Lee-Fists-of-Destruction harder.*

Between work, spouse, babies, work outside of work, and then those silly things like the need to sleep, who has time to go meet new people? And then actually go through the long, awkward process of *Friending.*

And the only thing harder than finding new friends post-college? Finding new couple friends post-college. Now four people to toss into the **Compatibility Blender.**

And the only thing harder than finding couple friends post-college? Finding couple married friends with young babies who:

A. Aren't on the fast track to divorce. So that by the time you finally go through all the awkward lunches, meet-and-greets, and you seal the friendship deal, one of them isn't off with their new assistant.

B. All four adults like each other, but the baby keeps slapping yours in the face and throwing temper tantrums like a spoiled teenager who gets a Kia for her first car instead of a BMW.

This twentysomething friend-shoot ain't easy . . .

Your 20s are about having the courage to write a frightful first draft.

I think most of us went into our 20s expecting a box office smash, when instead our twentysomething story is not even going to make it to the theaters. At least not yet.

As a writer, I used to be bummed about all the time and effort I spent writing hundreds of pages that would never see the light. But as I grew as a writer I learned that you have to write a lot of really atrocious first drafts before you can find the story you need to tell.

Our 20s are the same way. For many years it will be about getting words down on paper that we'll edit later. Plans will fail because that's part of **Frightful First Draftdom**. But five rewrites later, we'll lean back and say, "Wow, that's actually not too bad."

We have to be willing to allow ourselves to write some terrible first drafts.

You can't have a good story without a good struggle.

Don't ever, ever check Facebook when you're:

A. Depressed.

B. Drinking.

C. Depressed and drinking.

D. Unemployed.

E. Struggling with being *blessed with singleness* while some of your friends seem to be blessed with a Brad Pitt lookalike and that blazing white picket fence shining with the glory of the American Dream on steroids.

OR — F. Anytime after 9:17 p.m.

6

Life will never feel like it's supposed to.

When am I going to experience the success I am supposed to? I've asked that question exactly 4,399 times and only now am I catching a whiff of the answer.

Never.

Because what the heck is "supposed to"? Who holds the blueprint for my life—down to the number of kids, salary, and size of my house? Who decides "supposed to"?

"Supposed to" is a lie. A fairy tale. It is the stealer of peace and productivity. It is the leading cause of Obsessive Comparison Disorder with everyone who "has it better."

No one has it all figured out. No one holds their first child with all the answers. Not many walk right into their passion from the graduation stage. Not everyone gets married like they're "supposed to" or climbs the corporate ladder full of broken rungs.

If we keep trying to live other people's lives, who is going to live ours?

Being twentysomething can feel like **Death by Unmet Expectations**. However, you are right now, at this moment, exactly where you need to be. You'll just only be able to see that five years and thirty-three days from today.

Let go of "supposed to." Tie an anvil around its neck and throw it out to sea.

If we're always trying to live like we're "supposed to," we're never going to truly live.

7

Feel no shame in seeking help from a counselor or therapist. We all have rotting junk we try to wrap and hide under the Christmas tree. Get rid of it before it smells up your entire holiday.

There is nothing more depressing than searching for a counselor to help with your depression.

At 24 years old, depression was seeping under my bedroom door like a gas leak, and I had no idea who to call to help plug it up.

I mean, *find a counselor*? How does one go about doing such a thing? It's not exactly something you post on Facebook.

"Hey, does anyone have a good recommendation for a Thai restaurant downtown? Oh, and a good therapist who specializes in depression and an anxiety that feels like your heart has been injected with 1,500 milligrams of caffeine?"

And if finding a counselor who you connect with isn't hard enough, finding a counselor who you connect with and can *actually afford* is a miracle worthy of a burning bush crossing the Red Sea. Sure, *lots* of us twentysomethings have an extra $300 a month lying around for mental health. I just didn't happen to be one of them.

But we all need help. And sometimes the greatest help we need is help finding help.

Those friends who are uber-successful in their 20s are the outlier—not the norm.

If your friend is rolling around in that Range Rover or is posting pictures in front of that three-story mini-mansion, your friend either:

—Robbed a bank.

—Is making heavy withdrawals from their parents' piggy bank.

—Is making heavy withdrawals from Visa's plastic bank.

—Is part of the .02 percent Twentysomethings Club that are making heavy deposits on their own.

But remember, sometimes it's those who have the sleekest exteriors and the prettiest dining room sets who have the most garbage shoved in their closets.

9

Staying in a bad relationship is like letting your heart lie in the sun too long and then being surprised when it burns.

10

You grow INTO growing UP. (Part One)

HERE ARE 29 SIGNS YOU'RE . . . GASP . . . AN ADULT!

1. Ikea has become your Disneyland

2. Sleep goes from being your nemesis whom you avoid, to your best friend whom you wish would come over more often.

3. Watching three hours straight of your favorite show begins to feel *slightly* less productive than it used to.

4. You hear a baby crying and your first reaction is not to run, but to help.

5. If all the work emails you've read and written were placed side by side, they would cross the Atlantic Ocean. There and back.

6. 10:00 p.m. is late. 11:00 p.m. is dangerous. 12:00 is insanity. 1:00 a.m. is a fairy tale you remember hearing about in college.

7. Your body begins to ache from your vigorous *lack* of movement.

8. You begin discussions with *"Can you believe kids these days?"*

9. Debt goes from being this fairy tale to be repaid in a land far, far, away. To your daily reality show.

10. Memories of how you're going to feel Sunday morning actually begin to factor into your decisions on Saturday night.

11. **A Christmas sweater with a reindeer on it feels like a good idea. And you're not being ironic.**

12. You've mastered the interview *this is my dream job nod-and-smile* for a job you don't want and can't believe you're applying for.

13. **Facebook goes from being a hobby, to an obsession, to a chore you dread.**

14. **93 percent of the photos on your phone are of your baby or pet.** The remaining pictures are things you're trying to sell on Craigslist to make room for them.

15. You start cushioning all vacations with an extra day off for "recovery time."

16. Having lower lumbar support has become a major concern.

17. The thought of buying a new sofa or kitchen appliance makes you as giddy as a 12-year-old at a Justin Bieber concert.

18. You don't spend the week organizing your plans for Saturday night. No, organizing *is* your plans for Saturday night.

19. You haven't sprinted in two years. Something you realize too late as you try to dash across the street to avoid oncoming traffic, only to pull muscles you forgot you had.

20. **Classical music becomes this weird, welcomed breather.**

21. You have your first kid and realize what it's like to be young, be a parent, and have no clue what you're doing! And for the first time in your life, you actually begin to understand your parents.

22. **You don't have any kids. But you have two dogs or cats. Whom you treat as your kids.**

23. You're losing hair and gaining babies at an alarming rate.

24. You have a gym membership. That you've used twice in a year. One of those times was when you bought the membership. The other was when you tried to cancel it.

25. Your favorite movie and music posters are replaced by actual art. Granted, you purchased said "art" at Target or Ikea, but still.

26. You've caught yourself saying more than once, ***"I'm getting too old for this."***

27. Doing the dishes becomes your relaxing getaway.

28. You go to a college campus and wonder why there are so many high schoolers there. Then someone says you're actually looking at a group of college sophomores.

29. You now understand what your parents meant when they said, "You'll understand when you're older."

11

Lousy Jobs are The Twentysomething Rite of Passage.

We no longer send a boy into the woods with a spear and a prayer to kill a wild boar, have a vision in the clouds, and then come back a Man.

No, but I'd argue we still have rites of passage.

Armed with a coffee mug, twentysomethings are sent into the in-habitable **Land of Cubicles**, to see a vision in a computer screen, kill a few presentations, and come back a real.live.adult ready to make their contribution.

I've had a slew of sludgy jobs myself. But now, I am thankful for all the jobs I once lamented. It's because of them, not in spite of, that I've begun to enter into that sweet spot of my passion align-ing with how I make some moola.

However, before our chalice runneth over with thankfulness, let's shoot straight for a second.

Dung-Filled Jobs have always been around. My grandpa worked at a paper mill (dimly lit factory of hard manual labor) for thirty years, SEVEN DAYS A WEEK.

Our jobs mixing machiattos or encased in cubicles would've probably seemed a **Vocation Vacation** for millions from generations past and present.

Now please hear me, I'm not standing on **Henry my High Horse** yelling at you to *"buck up, pardner"* and stop complaining. I'm just reminding us all that it could be *heckuva-lot* worse. A little perspective can be powerful in making that sludgy job smell a little better.

So why am I now thankful for all my former jobs? Because **we can learn the most in the jobs we like the least.**

Take for example, my stint at a call center getting cussed out on the hour, every hour for something I couldn't fix or change. I wanted to quit every.single.day. But I was getting married in six months and couldn't afford a jaunt down **Unemployment Lane.**

However, through all the **Call-Center-Crud** I learned something vital—consistency. I learned to show up and do my work every.single.day. I learned to be patient, hold on, and just try to make it another time around the track.

So if you find yourself right now lost in a forest of computers and spreadsheets, not sure if you can make it another day, figure out what you need to learn there and learn it. If you don't, an assortment of lousy jobs might be your thirty, forty, and fiftysomething rite of passage as well.

LEARN. GROW. THEN GO.

See the vision of who you are and who you want to be, and then when the right time comes, run like that boar is chasing you.

12

Twentysomething life is "like a box of chocolates": you never know how awesome or atrocious it's gonna get.

Everyone dives into a box of chocolates with expectations.

High expectations.

You don't need to consult the snooty **Chocolate Legend** lying on the bottom of the box like it's **God's Gift to Chocolate Lovers**. I mean it's chocolate. You don't need instructions to consume chocolate. You've been mastering this your whole life.

So you grab that first **Round-Mound o' Goodness** your eyes behold and without hesitation, pop that bad boy in your mouth like a Mentos after eating garlic shrimp.

"*Ughhohmyuck!*" you can barely get out of your mouth, along with pieces of what you'd later describe, during therapy, as a crunchy-raspberry-mint-liqueur-licorice-ball of anything but chocolate.

How could chocolate do this to you? After all you'd been through together? You feel so cheated, so lied to.

Life in our 20s can feel the same way.

Who needs to consult that career counselor or coach, you've been doing life for 20-some years. You got it pretty well figured out.

Then you take that first big bite of your 20s expecting awesome, and are shocked when you're left with a mouthful of atrocious instead.

However, there's always a risk for a mess when you go in expecting the magnificent. There's always going to be imposters hiding among the incredible.

But the box of chocolates will redeem itself. Always.

Under one condition: you give it another chance.

13

IF YOU GREW UP going to church, at some point in your 20s you might stop going to church. If you grew up with faith as a central part of your life, at some point in your 20s faith might move to the outskirts of town next to the trailer park and three-legged squirrel refuge.

Your 20s are a process of making faith your own apart from your parents and childhood. Sometimes that means staggering away so you know what you're coming back to.

14

Don't go Into the Wild all by yourself.

Have you read the book or seen the movie *Into the Wild*? It's a true story of a guy named Chris McCandless, who graduates from Emory University top of his class, then leaves it all—his family, his savings, his car, safety, sanity, to go to Alaska to live on the land with little belongings or training.

He goes to the wild to escape all comfort and trappings that distract a person from finding truth. But as the movie progresses we also see he's escaping memories of an abusive dad, and as he changes his name to Alexander Supertramp, he's also trying to escape from himself.

Chris makes it to Alaska and lives in the wild. Then he becomes lost in the wild, then realizes he's truly alone in the wild, then trapped in the wild as the river floods and blocks his retreat. Then (the book came out in 1996 and the movie in 2007, so I think the *"Ruining the Ending" Statute of Limitations* has passed), Chris's final chapter is Death in the Wild.

Into the Wild wasn't an easy movie for me to watch. For many reasons. Mainly because I recognize some of myself in Chris McCandless, on a search for truth no matter the cost. I remember questioning, wrestling, doubting, and feeling very much alone.

And if you're in a very intense season or place of questioning, you know as well this can be a very lonely place. Sometimes painfully, undeniably, unrelentingly so. And there's something of strange importance that takes place in us when we are stripped of all the things that used to keep us company.

BUT DON'T ALLOW LONELINESS TO BECOME ISOLATION.

Don't pull your head inside your shell thinking only you can protect yourself. Don't go on a dangerous Great Alaskan Adventure to live off the land all by yourself. That's not a search for life, that's suicide.

WE NEED TO KNOW, AND TO BE KNOWN.

Invite a friend or two over for dinner. Talk, laugh once or twice—even if it's forced, and before the meal is over you might just notice your friends are chewing on the same questions you are. And at that moment of honest conversation, you will see light in the dark and dusty corners.

15

A college diploma is NOT your golden ticket into DreamJobLand.

It was a tad shocking when hiring managers frowned at my college diploma and resume as if I was handing them a used pizza box from a back alley Dumpster.

I learned that your college diploma is not your passport in. Your diploma is merely your **Pinky Toe in the Door**. It's the small sliver of light and the "*Okay, you've got one minute.*"

And what you do with that minute is the difference between crossing into *DreamJobLand* or traveling back to *LivinginYourParentsHouseAgainVille.*

16

Don't feel shame if at some point you join The Many. The Humbled. The Unemployed.

For a long time, I was an Unemployed.

I won't say exactly how long I was such; just that it was longer than William Henry Harrison's term as president and shorter than James Garfield's. (Thank you, Wikipedia.)

One day you're confidently *standing on*—the next, you're *laid off*. Your obvious expendability, slightly humbling. Like not playing in the playoff game and your team still winning 54 to 7 without you.

But hey, us *Unemployed*, we didn't like working that much anyway, right? Yes, maybe being an Unemployed is one of those blessings in disguise, an open window next to a closed door, a glass of lemonade produced from our severance package of sour lemons.

Maybe we've been given exactly what we've prayed for all along—our life back!

Now we have time to write that novel, hammer out that business plan, or find that lead guitar player for our band. Life is good.

———————

But if there's a "heads" on one side, there's a "tails" on the other. And unfortunately around the two-month-unemployed, still-can't-find-a job anniversary, the tail hits a growth spurt.

The novel hits a brick wall at page 51 and your ad on Craigslist for a guitar player only gets two responses. One from a thirteen-year-old who plays the violin in his music class, Tuesday and Thursday. The second from a guy named Rosco, who doesn't seem to really play any instrument whatsoever, but desperately wants to meet in person to "figure it out from there." Umm . . .

Then you go to a party and someone asks you for the 49th time, "Soooo . . . what do *you* do for a living," making sure to ask just loud enough for everyone to hear. A question that forces you to put on that **Conversational-Magic-Show** once again as you attempt to pull a rabbit out of your hat that died two weeks ago.

All that hope and excitement of a life with endless possibilities turns into lying prostrate on the couch watching a *Saved by the Bell* DVD set, getting angrier with every episode because *how can Screech be on television for ten years and I can't even get hired at Starbucks!*

Yes, being an Unemployed begins losing its luster, the shine turning quite dull. You can never truly relax, because you don't feel like you've ever done anything worth relaxing from. *Discouragement, Depression,* and *Despair* begin silently following you around like three sick dogs, jumping on your lap whenever you sit down.

———————

Finding a full-time job is the most demanding full-time job you'll ever have.

Except that it pays nothing. It's discouraging. And no one will care if you don't show up for work.

I learned to get up early, leave my house, dress nice, and treat my job search as a job.

If you stay at home and start "work" at 10:30 a.m. wearing your sweatpants, by 12:30 you might be downing a sleeve of Oreos and watching 23 Harlem Shakes on YouTube.

Giving everything you have to find the right job is the most important job you'll ever have.

God Save Us: The Many. The Humbled. The Unemployed.

17

Every time you write a rent check, an angel loses its wings.

Rent. Food. Health and car insurance. Cellphone bills. College loans. Trips to the mechanic to fix something in your car you didn't know existed. Yeah, these are all *wait-they-can't-be-serious* more expensive than when life was on parent-support.

Don't worry, the shock will wear off. But still, every time you write a rent check, an angel loses its wings.

18

A date is a date is a date is a . . .

A date is not a marriage proposal. It's not a romantic comedy. It's not a death sentence.

A date is a short period of time with another human being getting to know each other's story. Then you go home.

Don't make a date into something more than a date. Or you won't date.

Dating is simply about honing your taste.

If I asked you to describe your favorite whiskey, could you do it? Well, unless you're a mountain man named Gus or a hipster named Ivan, you probably couldn't because you haven't had much of any.

Same thing applies for dating—you can't really define what you're looking for in a guy or girl if you haven't spent time getting to know them. Each date gives you a better understanding of the complexity of your taste.

Dating is simply trial and error. And if you don't try, that will be the biggest error of all.

19

Our plans aren't the problem. Our timeline is.

I don't think our plans and dreams are the problem. Our *krizaaaazzzy* timeline of how quickly we wanted those plans and dreams to be sitting on our doorstep with a big Christmas bow is the problem.

I thought the red carpet was going to be rolled out on Day Three of life in my 20s when God had that penciled in for Day 2,334. You know, for when I was actually ready for it.

God has His timeline for your life. You have your timeline for your life. Some of the time those match—like on that one Tuesday in February, three years ago. But most of the time they don't.

We could try and hold tight to the *uncontrollable,* gripping the details of our lives like a five-year-old trying to walk a rhinoceros.

Or we can let them go and do their thing. We can drop them deep into the ground and water them with creativity, consistency, and patience.

Then when it's the right time, we'll watch our plans and dreams grow bigger, better, and more beautiful than we ever could've planned.

20

All job listings on Craigslist lead you to a warehouse in downtown LA "wearing something nice with shoes you can walk in."

Interviewing for a job you've never heard of and that you're not sure you can, nor want to do and then about halfway through the interview you're not really sure if you're even interviewing for a real job, is a **Proud Twentysomething Tradition**. If you can relate, congratulations! You're now a member of the club.

I once interviewed for a "sales" job I found on Craigslist and by the second interview I still wasn't quite sure exactly what I'd be selling. When the second interview ended I guess I gave the right answers about selling imaginary stuff because I was ushered into a room of twentysomethings where a large man who looked like Mr. Clean in a cheap suit gave us an intense speech about how much *money* we would make if we had the *passion to be sons of businessmen*, like him—all whilst sprinkling in a plethora of (lively) words like a sailor going through a hurricane.

At the end of his speech I asked if I could go to the bathroom. And I briskly walked out of the room, out of the building and to my car. (Okay, it was more of a scared scamper).

Selling is one thing. Joining Mr. Clean and his cult that bleepin' sells stuff is another.

Later that week I interviewed for a job at a learning center in LA to tutor Korean kids on how to take the SAT exam, a test that Harvard didn't exactly break down my door over my results.

When I arrived for the interview I was quickly ushered out behind the tutoring center in what could only be described as a back alley, as we then proceeded to talk about my job experience in between a Dumpster and a stack of wooden crates. I'd never battled the smell of rotten garbage during an interview before, so I think I was a little off my **Interview A-Game.**

Later that week, when I got the phone call that they "unfortunately" didn't have any open spots for me at the moment, I was extremely relieved. Because if they're showing you the back alley on the first interview, where do you go from there?

Twentysomethings interview for crazy, unheard of jobs. That just comes with the territory of little job experience slamming head-first into a stuck economy.

So if you're reading this right now and you can think back to your own *What-in-the-heck-just-happened* interview, *congratulations*, your membership card is in the mail. The club meets at 8:00 p.m. on Tuesdays at the Bowlmore Lanes. Tell Gladice at the front counter you're with us, and you'll get free shoes and fries half off. All night long.

21

"The key to success in your 20s is comparing yourself to everyone, every day. Then let that anxiety and fear propel you to work harder, faster, and with more motivation."

—Guy Who Had a Nervous Breakdown at 33

Nothing is more vital to twentysomething success than comparing yourself in every way, at every step, to everyone, both near and far.

Family, friends, acquaintances, enemies, *frenemies*, celebrities, co-workers—all are fair game, all are incredible motivational tools if you just allow yourself to study them at every angle and decipher how they have done their lives much better than you.

Pore over friends' Facebook profiles. Find all those your same age who have "Director" or "Vice-President" in their title. Go through every picture of their *My Life Is Awesome* Album. Measure how big their smiles are. Study their well-behaved kids. Figure out the square footage of their newly remodeled house.

Look at how nice their husband's suit is. Find the brand. Google it. See how much it must have cost.

Go buy a more expensive suit for your husband. Lease a Range Rover. Take a picture. Put it in your *My Life Is Awesome-er* Album.

We used to only be able to accomplish full-out, look-you-up-and-down comparison at our ten-year reunion. But now in the **Land of Internet** we can access it every, single, day. What a blessing.

Once you have studied, and obsessed, and found all the ways *THEIR* story is so much better than *YOURS*, you can use all this information as a motivator to smack your rear end into action like a jockey's whip on a racehorse.

Or don't.

Don't compare yourself to THEM.

You're not them. They're not you.

Your story doesn't fit in theirs. It'd be like watching *When Harry Met Sally* and then all of a sudden *Shawshank Redemption* cuts in. Billy Crystal making jokes as he crawls through a sewer pipe to escape from prison just doesn't quite have the same effect.

Don't cram YOUR PLOTLINE into someone else's story.

22

The grass is always GREENER on the other side, until you get there and realize it's because of all the MANURE.

23

Build the brand that is YOU.

What's your brand?

Have no idea? Email a few family and friends right now and ask them what words come to mind to describe you. That's your brand.

Everyone has a brand—it's simply who you are and who people think you are. Sometimes those are the same, sometimes they are miles apart. But intentionally knowing, crafting, and presenting who you are is crucial, especially in a competitive job market where a bachelor's degree has become the high school diploma. What makes you YOU?

Companies spend billions creating their brands with all roads leading back to one place—their website. It's open 24/7. It's the best billboard money can buy. And if you're going to their website, they have a better chance at getting a sale.

Likewise, as you build your brand, you should build **Your Own Website**.

Creating Your Own Website is the #1 biggest, baddest, and boldest amplifier of all job searching, platform building, brand-bolstering efforts.

Your Own Website is what a resume and power suit were in the '90s.

You need a website. Preferably a good one. Preferably something that looks professional or creative, depending on what you're trying to accomplish, and is engaging the career field you want to be in.

Take for example Lindsey Kirchoff's website "How to Market to Me." Lindsey started her website on how to market to Millennials because that's what she wanted to be hired to do.

And guess what, Lindsey was hired by marketing guru HubSpot to write about marketing.

What better way to prove to employers that you can do the job, than by doing it every day in a very visible, accessible way?

Employers can't see the story behind your 3.89 GPA.

Employers can see, taste, and touch a killer website.

Have no idea where to start? Talk to someone who does. Don't know anyone who does, ask **THE Google**. There's a million options that are cheap and will have you up and running in a day without any clue what HTML is.

Don't passively wait for a company to discover your potential. Prove it to them right now. Building your brand with a legit online presence amplifies all your existing personal branding, networking, job-searching efforts x 117.

Love is blind. Enlist some Seeing-Eye Dogs.

There are red flags galore waving in front of you. You're being warned there's a serious accident ahead, so why in the name of a **7-Car-Pile-Up** are you still driving directly toward it?

Enlisting trusted guides to help direct your relationship can save your life. A friend, a parent, a sibling, someone. You need help spotting the gaping potholes and oncoming traffic in your relationship that you can't see for yourself.

Love is blind. Don't move your relationship forward until you've enlisted some extra sets of eyes.

25

Your 20s will produce more failure than you'll choose to remember. The key is, when you fail don't begin calling yourself a failure.

Failing means you're simply finding a more profound way to be successful, if you're willing to learn from it, and then have the courage to possibly fail again. And possibly more profoundly than before.

We can't let failure be our death sentence instead of just one more sentence on the page before we turn it to the next. If we go for it, we will fail. We have to. That's part of lifting a weight heavier than you. You tear your muscles so that they can become stronger.

The only real *failure* of our 20s would be if we never had any.

Our imperfections, doubts, and questions about faith don't make us unfaithful freaks— they make us human.

As we begin The March of the Adult, our expectations of the crazy- successful, magically perfect life might be blown up like a hand grenade in a Hot Pocket. And with the explosion goes little things like our identity, dreams, friendships, faith, stability—you name it. **Life in our 20s can feel more time-bomb than tickle-fest.**

During this explosive time in my life I experienced a dramatic redefinition of my own faith. That's a polite way to say **I felt like a piñata getting the candy slammed out of me every day**— doubts and questions smacking me like a baseball bat in the hands of a freakishly large 7-year-old.

The biggest question I waded through every day—*does my life actually resemble what I say I believe?*

I wasn't sure I knew, or liked, my answer.

But where did I go to talk about it?

The place where I felt the least comfortable having an honest conversation about faith was church. When I stepped into a Sunday morning I felt like I entered some sort of problem-free parallel universe where everyone was so hyped up on coffee, donuts, lightshows, and Jesus that there was not a cloud, drop of rain, or speck of pollution in the sky.

I mean we all have problems, don't we? None of the churchgoers are immune to them—the pastor, reverend, rabbi, or priest included. If we were problem-free, why would we be going to church in the first place? **Why waste our time with church if we all share a collective perfection?**

So maybe at church and in conversations we should talk about, you know, what we *really* believe. Maybe we should just let our hair down a little, roll up our sleeves, and get our hands a little dirty with our doubts and questions. Maybe the church has trouble handling it sometimes, but God sure doesn't. Don't believe me, just read the Psalms.

27

Don't ever begin dating someone you met whilst in swimsuits.

Sure dating this person seems like an outstanding idea at the time, but your judgment, in many ways, might be a little impaired.

It might be exciting at the moment, but it's more likely to end in "*What did I do?*" than "I Do."

28

If at some point in your 20s you feel like you're six years old again...

... lost and alone at the San Diego Zoo, frantically searching for a familiar face—*hold tight,* you're experiencing a bit of a Quarter-Life Crisis. Stay put. Pray a lot. And in no time someone will call your name across the loudspeaker to tell you where you can be found.

Read these 22 signs you might be having a quarter-life crisis, and if you say "*oh my gosh yes*" more times than you say, "*this fool be crazy,*" then saddle up, partner. We'll ride these bumpy trails together.

22 SIGNS YOU'RE HAVING A QUARTER-LIFE CRISIS
1. You glare at your cat as you get ready for work and say, "*Gosh, I wish I had your life.*"

2. "Am I ever going to feel like myself again?" is something you ask. Every day.

3. A Bon Iver or John Mayer song comes on and you start crying. By yourself, or around friends. Or in the middle of a coffee shop as strangers hastily usher their children away.

4. You found this book because you *Googled*: Quarter-Life Crisis.

5. Visualizing yourself 15 years from now doing your boss's job makes you throw up a little in your mouth.

6. You're having arguments with your mom again about cleaning your bathroom and being home at a reasonable hour.

7. Your monthly routine of expenses being greater than your income is dawning on you as a serious problem.

8. You're having arguments with your newly cemented spouse and/or roommate that sound awfully like the arguments your parents used to have, that you swore you'd never have, yet are having.

9. You've moved six times in the last four years.

B. You've had six jobs in the last four years.

C. You've had six boyfriends in the last four years.

D. You've had six girlfriends in the last four years.

E. You've had no boyfriends or girlfriends in the last six years and you're scared your *boyfriending* or *girlfriending* is broken.

10. You'd pay top dollar for a moment of clarity.

11. Your temporary job at Starbucks has lasted three and a half years.

12. You find yourself repelled and compelled by church at the same time. You ask God for help one day and then you're yelling at Him the next. Your faith is a roller coaster and you're pretty sure your seat belt is about to come undone.

13. You see so clearly the two roads in front of you: a life of comfort and a life of risk. And you're not sure you have the right car or directions to go down either one.

14. You surf the Internet so much at work every day that you literally hit a point where you don't know what else to search for.

15. You laughed and cried when you first read *21 Secrets for Your 20s* on AllGroanUp.com.

16. Making a budget is completely debilitating.

> Even thinking about doing your taxes. Debilitating.
> Buying groceries. Debilitating.
> Doing dishes. Cooking dinner. Looking for a job. Calling your mom back. Calling your best friend back. Picking up the phone at all. DEBILITATING.
> So you watch four seasons in a row of _____, while Facebook-stalking exes and enemies.

17. The phrase you dread hearing the most at work is, "*Congratulations, you're getting a promotion.*"

18. Every time you're a bridesmaid or groomsman, a piece of you dies inside.

19. You dream about going back and slapping your *Smug-College-Self* who was so sure he had all the answers.

20. You seek out a mentor for answers one week and you avoid them like the 8th grader with bad BO, the next.

21. You have no idea where to go for answers.

Yet . . .

22. You're 99 percent sure a road trip would fix everything.

Do not confuse setbacks for settling.

Too many twentysomethings are miserable because we've confused setbacks for settling. That just because we moved back in with our parents or took that job answering phones, we're failures.

Sure maybe for the moment we've joined forces with a *not-so-brag-gable* life. Maybe we're not going to be a feature article in our alumni magazine anytime soon.

But we're not settling. We're visiting. This is a season, a stage, the perfect place in time for us to prepare to take the next needed step. You can settle for a season without *settling*.

You settle when you completely give up, when you let your dreams be suffocated by your current reality.

Visiting is simply a pit stop, and even though it might feel like the pits, don't let it stop you.

30

Where you fit in the Caffeine-Quadrants below will tell you a Grande-lot about your level of adultness.

KID AT HEART

Yes, you need your coffee in the morning but only if it's one-part black, three-parts fluffy crème brûlée creamer with a *scoche* of cinnamon, or one huge sleeve of hot cocoa mix you've hidden in your second desk drawer. You're caffeinating yes, while holding on to that **Sweet-Toothed Sweetheart** inside of you. And God bless you for it.

Sure, of course I'll play hopscotch with you at lunch.

SOPHISTICATED SUIT

You take pride in the fact that your Starbucks drink takes you a minute and thirty seconds to order.

You love when coworkers stop by your desk to ask you about your bottle of Yerba Mate infused with ginseng that you've proudly displayed like a trophy under your office lamp.

Any ogre can consume coffee like a Big Gulp. It takes an adult of refined sophistication to tailor caffeine intake like a well-crafted poem. You're as serious about adulthood as you are about your *triple pump, no-foam, upside-down, soy . . .*

MR. GRIZZLY ADAMS THE ADULT

You drink it black. Two days old if you have to. Brewed from your own pot that you haven't cleaned since Christmas 2009. You'd drink the stuff from a rusted tin can if it fit in your car's drink holder. Coffee is a means to an end, nothing more. Being offered frou-frou cinnamon swill is an insult to your hard-earned chest hair. You strongly believe that everyone who spends $4 a day at Starbucks should be deported to France.

You are Mr. Grizzly Adams the Adult. Get you a spreadsheet, talk radio, and a rock to sit on, and you're a happy camper.

DIET DOER

No coffee for you. Or high-fructose sugar syrup. No sir. You have your bottle of Diet _____. Zero Calories. No sugar. Three to seven times a day. Artificial sweeteners cascading through your veins as you pump out 60 minutes on the treadmill.

If anyone is looking for you they can find you full-steam, full-throttle, rocking adulthood M–F (with some small crashes and lapses, and times you eat raw cookie dough in the dark, in-between).

HERBAL HEALTHER

If it's not a tea and it doesn't contain spices from a hidden Asian island that only five people know how to get to, you're not drinking it. Oh you're an adult—a complex, mysterious one who listens to Yanni while meditating in the park.

THE NO-CAFFEINE

I don't know what kind of adult you are. And honestly, I don't want to know.

31

Faith is not a Mr. or Ms. America Contest.

Faith is not about having all the right answers. Faith is not about dressing up in your Sunday best and making sure every step is safe and elegant. Faith is not about presenting a body free of blemishes and scars.

Faith is to stop pretending like you have all the answers altogether, or that you even know the right questions.

Faith is walking in *as you are*. It is being stripped down to your bare essentials and simply saying, *here I am.*

Faith is not about impressing the judge to win a trophy. Faith is about standing there as the judge tells you that you're cherished and you have what it takes, blemishes and all.

Faith is simply hearing, and saying yes.

32

If at some point in your 20s you feel like you're all alone—you're not alone.

We're the most uber-connected, plugged in, engaged, informed, yet **Insanely.Isolated.Generation** in the history of the universe.

How can this be?

Is it because we're just simply not talking? I mean really talking, apart from Status Updates and Tweets?

Maybe it's just our culture's pastime to always appear like we have our *biznez* together, when it couldn't be further from the truth. To buy that convertible when you can barely afford rent on your small apartment. I'm not sure.

We've all experienced the frustration of our 20s going nothing as planned, so why do we still feel like we're the only ones who are struggling? This lie that we're all alone in our struggle is a powerful magnifier of depression, anxiety, and confusion in our 20s. It's vital we blow this ugly lie up.

So right now, if you feel like you're stuck between being adult and child, neither growing nor grown.

— you're not alone.

If you feel like you're struggling through a Quarter-Life Crisis you swore you'd never have.

— you're not alone.

If you're wondering when you'll ever feel like yourself again.

— you are not alone.

If you're searching for a place to hang up your coat because it actually feels like home again.

If you're staring at your gray, cubicle walls wondering how the heck you ended up here.

If you're wondering if God changed His number and forgot to pass the message on to you.

— you know what I'm going to say.

Call a friend. It's up to you to make the first move. Share war stories and strategies for dodging bullets.

You're not alone. And just knowing that fact can be enough to breathe life into that which has felt suffocating.

33

Just because you grow up doesn't mean you grow out of your insecurities. Sometimes, if you're not careful, you grow into them. Insecurities are *like Swamp Things*. Just when you think you've escaped, they rise up for a surprise attack.

In 8th grade, insecurity became a permanent fixture in my life. Like that 1970s oak entertainment center in your parents' living room—freakishly huge, yet it's been there so long you don't even notice it's there.

An acne attack kicked off my **Sweet 13 Insecurity Party**—acne of the face, chest, and back variety, all making themselves quite at home as my uninvited guests.

Then top that off with braces and love handles the size of Coke cans, and my *Insecurity* cruise ship was sailing through the choppy waters of puberty with a *Titanic-esque* chance of survival.

That's why I spent most of 8th grade under tables. As lights flashed all around and "Loveshack" boomed over the speakers at the school dance, I'd lie concealed by oversized tablecloth.

I'd picture all the popular girls desperately searching for me like their childhood dog had gone missing. And once they found me, *ahhhh yes . . .* they would sweep me out from under the table and parade me around the dance floor, showering me with kisses like a war hero just come back to the States.

But my homecoming never happened.

I wanted to be paraded as a war hero. Instead I just fought my own war.

THE INSECURE DISEASE

Even though insecurities stem from those things far in the past, they still have this strange, weird power to affect my present. Like a sci-fi movie, these ugly swamp things rise up and try to pull me into the mud. I thought I'd grown out of those insecurities. I thought they were dead and buried long ago, so why do they rise from their graves and do the tango right in front of me?

Maybe you feel the same. The abuse from your dad. The cheating girlfriend. The bully who wouldn't leave you alone. Just because you've escaped that situation doesn't mean its tentacles still don't poison you. No matter how perfect or perverted your childhood might have been, we all have shrapnel we need removed.

Unfortunately, I think many people as they grow up don't grow out of their insecurities, no they grow into the person they were always afraid and ashamed of becoming. Their insecurities and their identity get mashed together to become a multicolored ball of Play-Doh—no one being able to tell what was the original color.

Insecurities don't just disappear with age. No—they become more pronounced and ingrained. We must actively face these insecurities and work on removing the root, or the weeds will just keep growing back.

That's why we need help. All of us. A friend. A counselor. A mentor. A pastor. Seek help. Find support to face those Swamp Things in the eye and tell them, "You have no power or control over me any longer."

Attack your insecurities before they can attack you.

34

Sometimes the most proactive thing you can do is De-Plug.

I check my phone more times than a frantic smoker takes puffs after a six-hour flight.

Sometimes, I need to be off. Phone included. I need to sit and be still. To think. Reflect. Pray. Ask God to enter into my insane days for my own sanity.

Sometimes the most radical thing you can do is absolutely nothing at all.

35

Obsessive Comparison Disorder is the smallpox of our generation.

Nine out of 10 doctors agree this disorder is the leading cause to eating two boxes of Girl Scout cookies while watching *The Bachelor*.

So what exactly is Obsessive Comparison Disorder and more importantly, is there a cure?

OBSESSIVE COMPARISON DISORDER DEFINED

Obsessive Comparison Disorder is the disease I've coined to describe our compulsion to constantly compare ourselves with others, producing unwanted thoughts and feelings that drive us to depression, consumption, anxiety, and all-around joyous discontent. It's a habit from hades itself.

Like having to run outside to light up a cigarette, our addiction to comparing is uncontrollable and killing us with every puff.

HOW DO WE CURE THIS NEW FORM OF OCD?

1. Put on blinders

If you look at a horse that's carrying a carriage out in public, the horse will usually have blinders on. Blinders keep them from being distracted or freaked out by the noise of the peripheral. Blinders force them to focus on what's exactly in front of them, and nothing else.

We all need a set of blinders. We need to be **Forward-Focused**. What set of blinders can you put on that will help you look straight ahead?

If we took all the energy we waste comparing ourselves with those running next to us, how much farther could we run our own race?

2. Cut back on Internet and TV

Want to know a surefire way to cut your Obsessive Comparison Disorder in half?

Cut your Internet use and TV time in half. This is the best set of blinders money can't buy.

The Internet and TV takes your **Prius-Sized Comparison Problem** and turns it into a Hummer, guzzling energy for no good reason other than to try and look cool.

3. Celebrate What You Do

Celebrate what you do, whether big or small. Don't obsess about everything you don't.

Be inspired by others' stories but don't let their story dwarf yours. Don't let Obsessive Comparison Disorder devour with *Bubonic-Plagueness* creativity, energy, and peace—three vital characteristics you are going to need to rock your 20s.

We need to sail our own ship instead of drowning trying to swim to everyone else's.

36

Your 20s might be less about finding out what you want to do, and more about finding what you DO NOT want to do.

You're playing a game of **Emerging Adult Elimination**. Every time you cross something off the list, you're coming closer to naming a winner.

37

Awkward and coworkers go together like bad coffee and a break room.

Why is there so much awkward at work? Maybe it's because the maze of rainy-day-gray cubicles are set up like a ***D minus* science experiment** thrown together the night before the science fair. I'm not sure.

But the best part about having awkward coworkers? You have no idea just how awkward they are until you're fully employed.

LET'S TAKE A GANDER AT SOME OF THE TOP AWKWARD COWORKERS.

The MumbleCore

What was that, Henry?

The report is probably going to be eeldphterent

I'm sorry, I didn't catch the last part.

(*sigh*) I said probably it's an elephant monkey tattoo in the cupboard.

Did you say elephant-monkey tattoo?

(*huge sigh, with eyes rolling like bowling balls*)

And that right there is the best part about the MumbleCore—their sighs and rolling eyes are the only two things you can hear every time. Without fail.

The Quick-Clicker

You know they are browsing the Internet all day. They know they are browsing the Internet all day. Yet when you walk over to their desk, they click away faster than Billy the Kid at a shootout.

The One-Upper

You got a story you think is somewhat amusing? *Think again*. The One-Upper is ready to pounce at the first sign of a pause.

You saw three deer cross the street? He saw nine deer being chased by a mountain lion. You tripped down three stairs and cut your hand? *How cute*—he tripped down an escalator and was in the hospital for a month. You landed a $50,000 account; he landed one worth $5 million. You saw Paul McCartney at the airport. He saw John Lennon—after his death. And got his autograph!

The Shoulder-Rubber

You're locked in. Focused on a report. About to have a breakthrough when . . . *what in the name of* . . . there's two hands on your shoulders. And now . . . they're . . . rubbing.

You've been attacked by the Shoulder-Rubber.

Your best line of defense? Hunker down and pretend the report is so engrossing that you don't even notice those hands are there.

The Email-Only

Walking from their desk to yours takes exactly 23 seconds, if there's heavy hallway traffic. But the **Email-Only** wants to keep human interaction at a bare minimum.

The "That Won't Work"

Got an idea? *How nice.* The "That Won't Work" has five reasons your great idea is worse than filling your pockets with ham before walking into a lion's cage.

The Lingerer

He has no sense of beginning nor end.

The Lingerer lives, breathes, and has his being in the nexus of your doorway, never knowing when to say hello or when to wave good-bye. So he stands, obviously yet inconspicuously, weight on his left foot, hands firmly stuffed in his pockets as he intensely studies the picture of an elm tree on your wall like he hasn't examined it 332 times before, hoping that someone else will make the first conversational move.

You continue typing, pretending that you don't see him and if you don't finish your email in the next minute the world might EXPLODE!

But the Lingerer knows your game. He's the 8th grade guy who figures if he just hovers next to a girl long enough, maybe she'll just ask him on a date.

AWKWARD LOVES COMPANY

But the thing to remember is—the Lingerer or the MumbleCore, yeah, they think you're awkward too. And you know what, they're probably right. We all have our awkward uniqueness that makes us, well, *us.* Quirks are like birthmarks—you live with it for so long you kind of forget its there.

But gosh, 40 hours in the office would be boring if we didn't have the awkward to spice it up. When you leave this office and start a new job, it might be the amazing awkwardness you remember the most.

Complain-ism has become signature to our society—as culturally cool as deep V-necks and neon sunglasses. However, the Road To Miserable is paved with complainers and cynics.

Complaining is like a rash—too easy to catch, and tough to get rid of. I speak from experience. I'm a recovering "complain-a-holic" who's still trying to find the cure.

And I don't think it's just me. It seems that complaining, with a heavy dose of cynicism, has become our national pastime. It only takes three minutes on social media, talk radio, or the news stations to know that if you're not complaining about something, you're a bit of an outsider.

Complaining has become our social currency, our shared language used to form a mutual—if somewhat bitter—understanding of the world we live in.

We complain about our *unbearable* jobs, the slow Wi-Fi, our leaders in the office and around the world, and the waiter who brought only one basket of bread. The entire night!

But can we really be blamed?

For twentysomethings who walked off the graduation stage into a dark, deep pit called the Great Recession, how can we not lament our *great injustice*? For many, life has been more sour than it has been sweet. How do we not sing woes when trying to reap from fields ravaged with locusts and wildfire? Isn't lament a biblical concept?

The outlook may be bleak, but there are some who are choosing not to wallow but to walk confidently forward—a band of people who have chosen to follow another word, forcing cynicism on a raft and shoving it out to sea.

That word? Create.

Complaining and creating have a direct correlation. The more you create, the less you complain. The more you complain, the less you create. It's a pretty simple formula.

Instead of standing by the problem pointing out everything that's wrong, create a solution. Instead of ingraining an attitude of discontent, start working toward a new way forward. Create a movement, a relationship, a tool, or a conversation. **Do it big. Do it small. Just do something.**

Complaining is passive and powerless. Creating is proactive and powerful.

People gravitate toward Passionate Pursuers. On the other hand, people run like the plague from Complacent Complainers. It's up to us to create opportunity—instead of whining and waiting for one to float by.

What if we simply replaced moments where we had every "right" to complain, and created something instead? What would the world look like?

What if instead of termites, each one of us fighting to take our bite from the crumbling wood, we resembled millions of ants working together to rebuild our smashed hills?

The lyrics of a song by Gungor echo God's incredible creative capacity that He has also given to us: "You make beautiful things out of the dust." And for the hundreds of thousands of young people rising up today, the potential is astounding to do the same—to pick up the torch of the Creator and make beautiful things in a broken world.

Create. Make. Do.

Rinse. Repeat.

Create. Make. Do.

39

Attending weddings in your 20s is like going to high school prom all over again.

You don't know what to wear.

You eat an overpriced meal.

The dance is a little awkward, especially if you showed up without a date.

And the whole night you're slightly bummed you didn't get elected to the **Groomsman/Bridesmaid Royalty Court**.

40

You grow into GROWING UP. (part two).

HERE ARE 24 SIGNS YOU'RE ... *WHEW* ... NOT THAT ADULT:

1. The thought of becoming an *adult* makes you toss up a few *Fruity Pebbles*.

2. You see nothing wrong with still eating *Fruity Pebbles*. For breakfast, lunch, and dinner.

3. *TGIF* still means something more to you (*aka* you still watch your DVD set of *Boy Meets World* or *Step by Step*).

4. At the first sight of snow you hope *work* is canceled tomorrow.

5. You ironed your dress shirts for a month in your new job, and then decided a much easier strategy was to just stop believing that wrinkles exist.

6. You bring empty Tupperware to work to take home leftover office food.

7. You don't have kids. Or dogs. But you have a gerbil! Or you used to have a gerbil. What with the accident and all.

8. You've said *TMI* in the last week.

9. Come 8:00 p.m. you still have trouble telling the difference between hungry, thirsty, tired, or just bored. So you eat Little Caesar's and Skittles.

10. You're still a little miffed your parents turned your old bedroom into an art room/office. Seriously, did your time with them mean nothing?

11. You still *enjoy* your birthday.

12. You've stayed up until 3 a.m. at least once this week playing video games.

13. You spent an hour at work looking up Internet memes.

14. You know what an Internet meme is.

15. You still go to your parents' house to do laundry.

16. You secretly hope when you go to your parents' house to do laundry that your mom will do it for you.

17. And then you double-secretly-hope that while it's in the dryer she'll make you a sandwich and that dip you love.

18. You're still on your parents' cellphone plan.

19. You're still on your parents' car insurance.

20. You're still driving your parents' car.

21. You're back living in your parents' converted art room/office.

22. You think a 401(k) is a bike race down the West Coast.

23. You could sing five of the latest pop songs right now in their entirety.

24. You see a high schooler walking down the street and think, *Gosh, I want those pants.*

You're never too old for a nursery rhyme.

There was a young twentysomething who lived in a shoe.

She had so much debt she didn't know what to do.

She interned and hustled, without any luck.

Now she wakes up depressed, working part-time at Starbucks.

"My 20s were not supposed to be like this," she cried out in bed.

"I was Honors! I was tops! I was going to be a speaker on Ted!"

Lying there that night, hope was dwindling fast.

Her life of success, seemingly a dream from the past.

When all of a sudden from the window came a rattle.

Then a *famp*.

A ***KERPLAMP!***

And then a *zattle*.

"What the mustache?!?" she gasped, as little did she expect . . .

That *rat-tat-tatting* on the window was **Mr. Jeopardy himself, Alex Trebek!**

"Yes it is I, here in your room.

"I was summoned from sleep as I sensed such despair, such gloom."

"Yes, Mr. Trebek, nothing makes sense in my life.

"I thought by this age I'd be successful! Established! Heck, maybe even a wife.

"But my 20s have turned out nothing as planned.

"I feel stuck. Without answers. A lost girl in this land."

"Oh my dear, you see, they forgot to teach you this in school.

"But don't worry. We all go through it. Don't feel like a fool.

"As I always say, you need to find the right questions before you get to the answer.

"**Because life. Sometimes. Makes as much sense as the lyrics to *'Hold me closer tiny dancer.'***

"To be found, you must first become lost.

"To make a big difference, you must pay a ridiculous cost.

"Your 20s aren't as simple as receiving an A on a test.

"You have to come up with the right questions, and then you live out the rest.

"You must ask, 'who do I want to be?'

"It might seem a silly question, but its answer will affect your life, oh most profoundly.

"Because most people don't ask. They just do. And then never get undone.

"They work. And worry. They have little fun.

"But life is so fleeting like the petals on a rose.

"It is so beautiful, and then poof, there it goes.

"So I know things look bleak as you live in this shoe.

"But I swear, very soon, you'll know exactly what to do.

"You'll find your way around all the wrong turns and thorns.

"You've got too much going to not grab life by the horns.

"Just give yourself time. Neither Rome, nor Google, was built in a day.

"It takes hours of hard climbing and searching, but I promise you'll find the way.

"Just don't give up hope. That's what _overcomers_ do best.

"No matter their failures, they rise above the unrest.

"Because the key is perseverance. It's not sexy, but it's true.

"And I swear, very soon, you'll know exactly what to do."

A Quarter-Life Crisis might be the best thing to happen to you.

Yes, this turbulent season in your 20s where you feel like you're getting the insides ripped out of you like crab legs at a Las Vegas buffet. Yes, this season will be the most important season of development in your entire life.

Let me explain.

LIFE LIVED LINEAR

Growing up, we lived life so linear. Middle school. High school. College. Grad school. Cubicle job.

Climb that step so you can climb the next and the next and the next . . .

don't question. don't look back. don't turn.

Climb you fool. Climb!

higher.faster.farther.further.

We earn degrees, corner offices, 401(k)s—but is plodding up a stairwell the way we want to live?

TIME TO EXPLORE

A Quarter-Life Crisis is simply when you finally stop climbing the stairs and start exploring the unknowns of the 15th floor.

The door locks behind you. You strain your eyes but can only make out a dimly lit hall that appears to never end. You feel stuck in a Stephen King novel and at any second, train headlights might start hurdling toward you.

No syllabus. No textbook. No professor with a flashlight to shed light on all the answers.

No, just you and an endless amount of rooms.

All you can do is start opening doors.

And it's a tad terrifying, if you're honest. Because exploring the dark has always been that way.

Because you'll enter rooms that smell like mothballs and old pee.

Because you'll get lost and there's no assurance that you'll ever find your way out.

VALUE OF A QUARTER-LIFE CRISIS

But the more rooms we go in, the more the maze begins to make sense. Exploring in the dark is not easy. But our eyes begin to adjust. We start learning how to really see.

We learn how to fail.

And struggle.

And persevere.

We learn that sometimes life will dismantle you so that you can be rebuilt.

We learn how to explore again like we're eight years old in the field behind our house.

We might look back to our life on the stairwell and realize it wasn't much of a life after all.

So yes, I'd rather we experience crisis now and have the rest of our lives to live than when we're 55 with so much of our lives already cashed in. I'll take my quarter-life crisis now rather than when three kids, a mortgage, and spouse are at stake.

Really our quarter-life crisis is a period of transition when everything that used to be familiar becomes very unfamiliar. And if we don't learn how to explore now, then we'll *really* be lost later.

The most dangerous job you can have in your 20s is a comfortable one.

Comfortable is quicksand—the job you never wanted becoming the job you can't escape.

Worse than no-job, frustrating job, or a demanding job, is a job that demands nothing. Like taking basket weaving your senior year. Sure you'll get an easy A, but what did you miss out on in return?

There is a stark cost for time wasted on comfortable. You don't learn. You don't refine who you are or what you're capable of. Remove challenges, remove growth.

Here are two signs your job might be *La-Z-Boy-esque* and it's time to escape.

1. YOU FEEL DRAINED BY DOING NOTHING

If you come home absolutely drained from work and need to watch 2–4 hours of TV a night to escape. Then you think back to your day and realize you really did nothing at work. You're really just drained because you're experiencing the effects of **Mushy Mind**. You're drained because you've mastered how to spread one hour of actual work over a span of eight.

Being drained by comfortable is an uncomfortable way to start living. Because it's incredibly hard to escape. Like a carousel ride that never stops spinning. Jump and roll.

2. "WE WANT TO PROMOTE YOU" IS THE PHRASE YOU FEAR MOST.

If the idea of being promoted makes you more nauseous than the time you ate cotton candy and three churros before jumping on the **Spinning Teacups of Terror**, then why are you working there?

I can hear lots of "*but Paul, you still don't understand . . .*"

No, I do understand. **Comfortable is your drug. I'm checking you into a clinic.** Quit comfortable before it's too late.

The Freshman Fifteen is nothing compared to the Cubicle Cincuenta.

Cubicles are where waistlines go to die.

Unfortunately I learned this the hard way. Because there's one inevitable truth about offices where people don't really like their jobs.

They eat. A lot. And I'm not talking carrots and cucumbers.

No, we're talking about the office birthday cake.

The Christmas potluck singalong.

The July 4th Barbeculooza.

The "Just Because" Donut Day.

Basically any work-related Food-a-Thon where everyone tries to drown their jobs for 30 minutes with chocolate icing.

Just say no.

Don't let office birthday cake be forced on you like a cigarette behind your middle school. Don't sit at your computer perched like a Roman gargoyle.

Bust out before your belly does.

In case you were wondering, cubicles don't make sense to anybody other than upper management.

I would be willing to bet that only 13 percent of all "Cubicle Americans" actually have a positive outlook on life. And half of that 13 percent is probably stealing from their company.

46

Dates are supposed to be awkward.

Dating is like riding the tilt-o-wheel at a local carnival—nauseating, rickety, and about halfway through you'd pay anyone $20 to let you off.

For most of my 20s, this pretty much summed up my feelings toward dating. It looked like a good idea from afar, but the moment I was getting strapped in, I felt like I ate too much funnel cake.

But now, married with two babies, I look back at the good, the bad, and the awkward of dating, and I now better understand and appreciate the value of the process.

If 97 percent of your dates are horribly awkward, you're right there with 97 percent of the population. Awkwardness and dating go together like Hugh Grant and romantic comedy.

Plus, how else are you going to have incredibly awesome stories to tell your friends and family later? **Awkward First Date Story = Social Gold.**

Don't worry about being in the wrong job. Worry about your job getting the wrong you.

When you're a vagabond writer, coffee shops are your home and I've definitely seen and experienced my fair share of angry, disgruntled, bitter coffee shop workers, and frankly who can blame them. If I had to take orders all day from the Real Housewives of O.C. who order with extreme rapid annoyance their (wish this was a joke) "Grande in a Venti cup, half-caf, 2 1/2 shot, ristretto, 2 1/2 pump sugar-free vanilla, half non-fat milk, half soy, 191 degrees Fahrenheit with three ice cubes, no foam, upside down, stirred, 11 Splendas, caramel on top, on bottom, and on the sides of the cup, with a strip of whipped cream, sprinkled with vanilla powder, skinny caramel macchiato, in a pre-warmed for-here cup"— I'd tell them to shove every single penny of my $8.25 an hour.

THE MAYOR OF STARBUCKS

But it's crazy packed at the Starbucks I'm writing at on this one day, and the guy making the drinks his hands are flying to keep up. And as he's making all these drinks, a thirtysomething lady is telling him an in-depth story, and somehow he's making drinks, smiling, and saying, "Yep. Wow. You don't say . . . *Fred your skinny caramel macchiato is ready at the bar* . . . Wow. Yep. That's amazing . . ."

Then to my disbelief something begins to happen that I've never seen in all my thousands of hours spent in coffee shops. The thirtysomething lady finishes her story, says goodbye, and the 45-year-old businessman, who already got his drink, steps up and begins talking to the guy making drinks as two people wait behind him holding *their* drinks.

These customers weren't waiting for their drinks; they were all waiting for their chance to talk to the guy *making the drinks*. I'm pretty sure if anyone would've taken a picture of me they would've caught a stellar prolonged shot of **Mouth Fully Agape.**

Then I start wondering how many of these people bought a drink just as an excuse to come talk to this guy who apparently is everyone's best friend.

Later in the day when this Starbucks employee is walking around the store cleaning up, he literally can't walk two steps before someone is calling his name asking him to join their conversation. And I see more why this guy is so loved. He's laughing and looking people in the eyes. He's telling stories and more importantly listening intently to all of theirs. He's not cheesy and over the top. He looks and sounds like he actually cares.

I mean really, what's with this guy? Is he that special? I wonder if I should stop the guy myself and ask for his autograph. Because I feel as though I'm in the presence of the **Mayor of Starbucks.**

WHAT'S THIS DUDE'S STORY?

How can this Starbucks employee be making such an impact? Does he really love working at Starbucks that much? I mean he's no young kid, maybe late twenties, early thirties and he doesn't seem like the Starbucks-lifer type either. As I watch him continue to do his thing, I begin imagining this guy's story, thinking about what maybe led him here.

Maybe this guy had a good job selling Priuses or new homes or something, but the Great Recession and a jerk of a boss kind of did him in. Maybe he got into a little bit of debt and there in his late twenties he kind of just had to hit the reset button. Maybe he even moved back into his parents' house and was living in the basement. Yeah, and maybe he can't really afford a good car so he drives around in an old car that can only go for two miles before it starts to overheat. And yet, the car has no working heat. It overheats but has no heat. Of course! And that's something to imagine because we are in Colorado and it's frigid-freezing outside.

I'm doing what writers do and I'm making up this elaborate, crazy story about this guy who really doesn't want to be working at Starbucks at all and yet is making this big impact in people's lives, and then I notice him limp a little.

Oh yeah, and this guy only has one leg too! I'm giggling to myself now because I'm creating a Hallmark character here. This story is way too good, way too unbelievable to be true.

I sit there amazed.

And severely convicted.

Because the whole story *is in fact true*. Even the part about him having one leg. Because the Starbucks employee is my brother. And if anyone knows his story, it's me.

I know that my brother struggles going to work most days, especially when it's 4:00 a.m. and his alarm clock is going off. And

I know that standing up all day on his prosthetic leg hurts him more than he'll ever let on. And I'm sure that some days he wishes he was working somewhere else. Yet a long time ago and then every single day since, he's made the very intentional and radical decision to bring the very best of him to work, even though his work is not always the best.

All my complaining, all my excuses and justifications on why I deserve to give my job 50 percent because I've decided it's only 50 percent my dream job, well, those excuses don't seem to stand for very long next to the Mayor of Starbucks.

The biggest surprise about becoming an adult that no one ever talks about . . . Adulthood. Never. Stops.

Growing up in school we were conditioned to live in defined periods of time. Push ourselves for a semester, pull some all-nighters, cram, chug a six-pack of Mountain Dew and wear our pajamas for three days straight, take those grueling finals, then *bam*. You're selling your books back for $17.33, driving across country—on to summer break, on to something new, on to a complete change.

Adulthood is the opposite. It's the Energizer Bunny—it just keeps going and going and . . .

49

Every breakup has two breakups. I'm no physicist, but this is a law of physics. Of this I am certain.

Yes, you'll have the first tearful "*It's over*" sitting in the front seat of your Honda or on a park swing. Then 1–2 months later after there's "*been talk,*" you'll have the "real breakup" because she forgets to call like she used to or he checks out the waitress like he's a judge for Miss USA. And gird those loins because in the second breakup there will be a lot more breaking.

50

God in His infinite mercy saves us from Syllabus Syndrome.

If I had a half-dollar for every time I cried out to God for Him to show me the plan, I'd be in the Guinness World Records for my extensive coin collection.

But I realize now that God saves us from *The Plan*.

Thank God He didn't show me the syllabus for my 20s.

If He would've showed me all the assignments my 20s were going to entail, I would've been crushed by it. I would've dropped this whole decade like a calculus class and never returned.

God gives us what we can handle, and sometimes that means not giving us the exact thing we cry out for the most.

51

Once you've officially broken up you have to "break" away from the hundreds of memories, feelings, and familiarities of what used to be.

After the official "second" breakup, when it's really over, comes the heavy lifting of really *really* breaking up. You've broken up with the person, but now you have to start cutting all the strings that are attached and intertwined.

And I don't need to tell you that this is where the *real breaking* of breaking up happens. It might take more time and tears than you'll ever want to admit. But there will come that morning when you'll wake up, and it will be over. This time *for real* for real. And the funny thing is you won't even notice. Because the moment the breakup is *really over* is the moment you stop wondering *when is this ever going to end.*

52

Your ability to learn Wine 101 might be the difference between eating at the Adults' Table or stuck in a folding chair with the kids.

Wine. It's what adults drink. Preferably while listening to music that you'll hear the next day going up an elevator or in a dentist's office.

Even if you have no desire to drink wine, if you're going to join the **Adult Major Leagues** you might need to learn how to *talk* about drinking wine.

WINE 101

Wineology is like chemistry class. You won't understand a thing at first, but just as long as you don't mix too many of the wrong terms together, hopefully nothing will blow up.

Think I'm exaggerating? Pop quiz hot shot.

Do you like your wine smoky? *Dry*? How about with floral accents or a flourishing bouquet? Maybe you want it cedary or grassy?

Intimidated? Don't you worry that **Baby-Bottomed Face**. If you're not quite sure how to talk about your wine yet, that's okay. Because how you hold your wine might at least help you fake it through the night.

It doesn't take a connoisseur to know you don't dare place wine in a red plastic cup. And don't even think about pouring it in that gleaming souvenir goblet you bought at Medieval Times. That screams amateur hour.

No, your Wine Chalice must be long and elegant, and you must cup the basin of the glass like you're holding a frightened bird that just fell out of a *cedary* tree. Not too hard lest you might hurt the bird, but not too loose that you let it fly away.

And whenever that **Wine Wizard** cometh your way asking you about the earthy undertones, **do not panic**!

Simply stare at the glass and move it around in three tight circles like you're trying to rock that small, scared bird gently asleep. Then hold the glass in front of your face like you're inspecting its broken wing. Sigh slightly, yet contently, like you've just identified the place of wing displacement. Tilt your head at a 20–30 degree angle, nod, and then take a small, prolonged *experience*.

That's the cork to a bottleful of any proper Wineology. Your future in-law will be patting you on your shoulder and asking your advice on his stock portfolio before you can even say nutty.

53

Terrible jobs and bad leaders go together like bowling and fried food.

Bad leaders strut around the office like peacocks, displaying their bad habits in full color.

But you know what, we can learn as much from bad leaders as we can from the good. Begin writing down all the things your not-so-splendid boss does that you swear you won't repeat. Someday you will be called to lead. Start formulating your vision now of how you will, and won't, do it.

54

In the working world, very rarely is someone waiting there to teach you how to do your job. They're expecting you to teach yourself.

I didn't really understand that for years I'd been paying my professors a big wad of cash. Sure, I didn't give professors a handshake like a mobster paying off a politician, but I was paying big money to sit there and be taught. Of course I didn't appreciate it at the time. I didn't realize how rare it is to have a professional in your field dispensing wisdom like a gumball machine.

Because we're not paying them any longer. No, no, they're paying us.

55

If you want to be taken seriously as a twenty-something professional, here are fourteen office/cubicle Must-Haves that will transform any Coffee-Fetcher Frog into a Corner-Office King.

1. A BIG clock—and not one that uses simpleton numbers, but is engraved with intellectual Roman Numerals. As someone jaunts into your office, they will stand at attention and know that your time is important, and most likely, much more important than theirs. And if you can also get a GIANT clock that displays time from different parts of the world, now they'll know your time has even reached International Status.

2. A midsized statue of any predatory-type or behemoth-sized animal perched on the front of your desk like it's ready to

pounce. A mouse or cat won't do. No, you need a giant hawk or bear swooping on an unsuspecting fish. Then if any disagreements arise in your office with **Sam the Simpleton**, you can stop and stare at the statue, then back at him as if to say, *one of us is the bear, the other the fish. Need I say more?*

3. Don't even think of bringing in that college photo collage adorned with red cutout hearts. No, you need two–three personal photos on your walls, max. One of them of your significant other or kids. The other of you shaking the hand of a celebrity. That way your coworkers know when you offer them a handshake, you are offering them the **Hand of Legends**.

4. Any **Joe Schmo** can have a computer in their office. That's *so 2000.* But two computer screens, side by side, with one of them preferably the size of a large flat-screen TV. Now we're working. You have so much **Important-Ness** on your computer you need a home-theater system to contain it all.

5. A desk space that looks like you have a **Mini-Mr. Clean** living in your drawer who comes out at nights.

6. A framed Motivational Poster about the secret to being successful. This screams **I Am the Office Sensei** and I work on a higher plane than you.

7. A fat, shiny, silver pen on your desk. *You don't even want to know how many big deals I've signed with this **Ball-Penned Bad-Boy**.* No seriously, if I told you, your **Sales-Assistant-Self** would cry.

8. A coffeemaker. And not your secondhand Mr. Coffee from storage. No, we're talking an espresso-pressing, latté-making, **NASA-Commissioned Contraption** that says, "I'm cool and I'm caffeinated. Try to slip something past me, I dare you."

9. A mini-fridge under your desk. This says: *I don't waste company time searching for a midday meal.*

10. A Big Black Leather King's Throne that puts you three feet higher than anyone else, sitting behind your solid mahogany table imported from Tibet. And a **Triple Bonus Score** if there's a rumor around the office that you might have a red button under your desk.

11. A serious newspaper like the *Wall Street Journal* or top industry magazine, preferably worn just enough to say, "Go ahead, ask me what's on page 54."

12. A small side table that is solely reserved for awards, framed diplomas, certificates, pictures of you glad-handing VP's, all with cultural artifacts sprinkled sparsely in between from exotic places like Thailand or South Africa. *Oh I'm sorry, did you forget how important I am?* **Have you not beheld my Side Table?**

13. One large potted plant to prove that you can make anything flourish in tough conditions.

14. A **Complex Contraption from the Year 2050** that moves, oozes, swings, turns, or balances. *Yes, I can spend large sums of money on something that has no functional purpose. And yes, I possibly have the power to travel in time.*

56

Watch out. "Official Adults" might stereotype you for being twentysomething.

Generational stereotyping is all the rage these days. For some reason we think a generation can be summed up with a two-paragraph label like a box of Wheat Thins.

If you feel like you're being stereotyped because of your age, your best ally is **quiet confidence**—a humble consistency that shows up and gets the job done. You don't argue with them about your skill set, you just show them every single day how awesome your skills are.

It's a tough, thankless gig, but soon, very soon, you'll prove to them that **you're a person, not an age range.**

57

Don't be Smothered in Twentysomething. We need to sweeten our lives with some Generational Potpourri–a collection of age ranges with different backgrounds and experiences to spice our lives up.

Many of us twentysomethings love talking to each other about **The Problem**, without realizing that we're all seeing **The Problem** from the exact same angle, which becomes **The Biggest Problem** of them all. We need some different perspectives.

We need the wily old vets in our lives getting all kinds of profound and grizzled on us.

And we need some young kids in our sphere to remind us that the smallest things in life can be outrageous and fun.

Let's quit living like we're the lead role in **The Twentysomething Sitcom** and if any older person makes an appearance it's only for comic relief.

Let's stop being **Twentysomething Pod People**. That has *B-movie-straight-to-DVD* written all over it.

58

Everyone is too busy putting a PR spin on their own lives to care too much about yours.

Want to know the secret of what the majority of people care about the most?

Themselves.

Their appearance, their profession, their future, their **LPA—Level of Perceived Awesome**.

People pore over their lives, reading the fine print and dissecting every detail. They only give your life a cursory glance.

We spend so much energy worrying about what other people think, when honestly they're not really thinking about us at all.

We spend so much time making our lives look virtually appealing, when maybe we should spend more time, you know, *actually making our lives*.

Don't live for them. Live for you. Focus on achieving your own Personal Records and not on posting your own PR.

59

The most ridiculous thing you can do as an adult is stop being ridiculous.

Taking yourself too seriously is very serious work. Very important, steadfast, I-can't-be-bothered business. Where you save up every penny to buy a one-way ticket to *Boredullameville*—it's kind of like living at Disneyland, except the exact opposite.

And there at *Boredullameville*, you can even be the mayor. You can fret over your reports. You can wear slacks and use big words. You can prove the magnitude of your intellect with every "But the data says otherwise." You can give projects to subordinates and never look them in the eye. You can talk policy, procedure, and protocol all the livelong day. You can send out fiery emails perched behind your big oak desk, *ccing* the whole village. Yes, you can be Mayor of *Boredullameville* and there spend your days living a very efficient, never-change-lanes-cruise-control life. You can make as much waves as a dead, dry leaf falling into a puddle of water. It's awesomely un-awesome.

Or you can live differently. You can live ridiculously.

The #1 rule to living ridiculously? Never, ever, under any circumstances, worry if people think you're ridiculous. Ridiculous people don't even know where *Boredullameville* is on the map, let alone have any desire to run for office there.

Haters love to hate. Boring people love to bore. The realistic live all too real. Naysayers love their ample amounts of nay.

On the other hand, ridiculous people live with their bodies dipped in awesome and they don't care who crawls out from under a rock to tell them that painting your body in awesome is not the appropriate or responsible use of resources.

Ridiculous people are these weird, wild people that actually **make you feel alive**. They take one step in the room and the heavy weight of *Stuffy Adult-Dom* floats away like a helium balloon.

Ridiculous people believe in others more than others believe in themselves. Then they constantly encourage others to see the truth that they see.

Ridiculous people don't care much for facts. Oh, they take them into account, but they know facts aren't always factual. They know that facts are contrived by self-proclaimed adults for their own fancy.

Ridiculous people care more about doing what's right than what will look right to others.

I want to be ridiculous. Are you with me?

60

Our 20s are not about finding home; our 20s are about finding the right place to build it.

You know when you're coming back home from a really long trip, the plane has landed, and you text "*I'm here!*" to that someone important enough in your life to come pick you up at the airport. Which, on the **How Real Is Our Relationship Scale** is slightly above picking up the tab at lunch and slightly below assisting on a cross-city move. To a 4th story apartment.

Buzzing with nervous excitement, you're barely able to restrain yourself from throwing off your seat belt and being **That *Guy*** who pretends he doesn't understand English as he tries to cut in front of 15 rows while flustered flight attendants scold him over the loud-speaker.

But as you fidget in your seat, the excitement begins to wane as your plane taxis for so long you worry the pilot accidentally took a wrong turn and is headed back to New Jersey.

And then the plane finally stops and the pilot makes an announcement that this flight is fourth in line to deplane.

And as you're still debating to yourself whether or not "deplane" is actually a word, *De Plane* rolls slowly forward like they landed on a runway full of wet cement.

Then finally the seat belt light disappears as excited travelers compete for the coveted award of **Eat It! I Stood Up First**.

And as you stand in that awkward **Close Encounter of the Plane Kind**, where you're half-crouching beneath the overhead compartment, straddling the side of a seat and your carry-on, the pilot comes on to tell you that the door is malfunctioning and a special crew is being sent from Newark to come fix it.

A collective groan rises to the heavens.

Then they finally get the door open and back in seat 545F you can see some dots of people looking like they are getting off the plane, but then you notice that every person in front of you is over 77 years old and has somehow fit several full-sized oak tables in the overhead compartment that they're now trying to unwedge. Without much success.

And there, straddling 545F, running your hands through your hair, clutching and unclutching your bag as you try desperately not to become the **Unidentified Crazy Person** who shows up on the 11 o'clock news, you begin to seriously lose hope that you'll ever make it home.

Yeah, unfortunately life in our 20s can feel the same way.

Your plane has landed, you're ready to get off and go home, but the de-plane-ing process takes 4–7 years. And once you get off you realize you're actually in the wrong town, and home is 2,321 miles due west.

Sound depressing? Yeah, it kind of is. Let's be honest.

Because your 20s really aren't about jumping off the plane and going back home. The life of a twentysomething is that of a nomad. Picking up your tent and continually traveling to locate the herd and test the soil so that you can find the right place to land, the right place to call home.

Your 20s are not about finding home; your 20s are about finding the right place to build it.

61

College is learning all the techniques and theories on how to dive. Graduation is stepping up to the edge and taking the plunge. The rest of your life is spent learning how to swim.

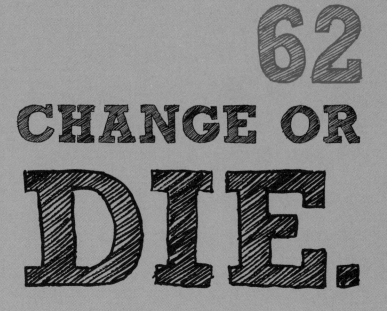

62

CHANGE OR DIE.

Most twentysomethings have experienced a near decade of transition with more job and housing changes than a chameleon has colors.

Change has been thrust on us like a blind date—we didn't want it, but through the experience we learned something important.

We've had to change, morph, become better and more resilient. The lack of a red carpet has forced us to find a different, better way to the party.

It's always been true that those who know how to change will win. If you master the **Art of Change**, I see YOU with a big grin, holding the trophy.

63

Breaking up is like a fire. It destroys. A lot. But sometimes it's beneficial and necessary, like a farmer taking a field overgrown with weeds and setting it ablaze.

You'll learn more about love in the wake of a "fiery" breakup than you ever will watching a romantic comedy.

If you allow the fire of a breakup to burn through the dead weeds in your life, the plants that will grow back will reap tons of sweet fruit.

Don't become a member of the Real Live Half-Dead Adults' Club.

What do I mean? Well to explain let me take you to a call center.

CALL CENTER CRISIS

In my opinion, the only difference between hell and a call center is the phones. (Unless the devil is sporting a cellphone these days.)

When you work at a call center you realize fairly quickly that when people call in it's not because they want to chitchat or tell you about the amazing work your company is doing.

No. They call because they have a problem. A life-shattering, comets-colliding, worlds-imploding problem that you're to blame for.

And since our call center was wildly understaffed, every person I spoke to was usually waiting on hold for *an hour*. Oh, they were just as pleasant as a peach come summertime by the time they got to me.

THE CALL CENTER CHEF BEHIND ME

The only really nice thing about working at the call center was the solidarity and unity among coworkers based on one simple truth—we all hated our jobs. Every last one.

But then I'd ask coworkers how long they'd been working there.

"Five years," they'd say.

"Five years!" I'd respond. "Well, when did you first start hating the job?"

"Five years ago," they'd say.

"Five years?" I'd respond.

Something about these conversations didn't make sense.

Take Rosey who sat behind me. She was about 45 years old, kind, energetic, and was an amazing chef. The office parties where she brought carrot cake were the only times all calls were placed on hold.

But Rosey had been working at the call center for a long time and complained about the job with the same frequency as the incoming calls.

"Rosey, why don't you quit this lousy job and pursue cooking?" I asked. "You're an amazing chef. You hate it here. Why stay?"

"Oh, I tried pursuing cooking once," she said. "But it was hard. Didn't pay enough, you know? And I couldn't catch a break. So I gave it up and started working here."

"Well, I think you should give it another shot," I said.

"No, no. That's not for me anymore," she said putting on her headset. "I'm done with dreaming. Just gets your hopes up for no good reason. You're young, but one day you'll learn. Sometimes you've just got to say goodbye to the fairy tale and put on your grown-up pants."

Right there at that moment, I vowed something. **I was never going to wear grown-up pants**.

You see, the call center was filled with *real-live-half-dead adults*—people who are more comfortable with cruddy than they are with making a change for the better.

They were fine living crudfully ever after. I was not.

There's too many *real-live-half-dead adults* for you to join the ranks. So if at some point you want to accidentally drop your "grown-up pants" in a real.live.fire, you have my blessing.

65

Know when your sad season is over and you just need to stand up and dance.

I think some of us forget how NOT to be sad.

We become so used to being stuck in a funk that we don't know how to un-funk. Those sad songs that held us during all those long nights alone, stuck on repeat because they've been the only friends we have known.

Now, don't get me wrong. I love a good Bon Iver, Band of Horses, Ryan Adams, Death Cab for Cutie playlist as much as the next twentysomething. The kind where you feel transplanted into the middle of a drizzly Seattle day, sitting on a forest stump drinking espresso and wrestling with life's hardest questions. *What could be better?*

But I think many of us artificially keep ourselves in a funk because we keep listening to the same sad songs over and over and over—literally and figuratively.

Sometimes you just need to thank Bon Iver for your time together, but it's time for you to go. You need to buy a one-way ticket and fly toward some sunnier skies.

It's time to change that playlist.

Possibly everything we needed to learn about being successful as adults we learned from playing Oregon Trail and Where in the World Is Carmen Sandiego?

"Class, put your books away. It's time to play Oregon Trail." "Everybody partner up and jump on a computer. It's time for Where in the World Is Carmen Sandiego?"

Were there sweeter elementary-school sentences? The promise of Oregon Trail or Carmen Sandiego would fill my little body with waves of excitement like I'd just caught the winning touchdown at recess while simultaneously downing ten Pixy Stix.

The journey from Missouri to Oregon or jet-setting around the globe huddled around that gray Apple computer was a glorious one.

But as I look back, what did we really learn from playing these games? Were avoiding dysentery and knowing our limitations on how much buffalo we should shoot really necessary life lessons?

Or did these games teach us something more? Maybe we learned complex and profound truths about how to be successful in our 20s that we can still benefit from today. Sound crazy? I say nay.

SEVEN LIFE-CHANGING LESSONS OREGON TRAIL AND CARMEN SANDIEGO BESTOWED UPON US

1) Planning ahead before you start on the trail is key.

I loathed going through the initial process of setting up our wagon, picking your profession, stocking up on supplies, and choosing the best time of the year to leave. Just give me a gun and put me on the trail so I can start shooting squirrels.

But without fail my lack of planning would leave me stranded somewhere in the Rockies in the freezing winter without extra clothes and a busted wheel. (What 4th grader thinks about stocking up on wagon tongues?)

Most of my post-college experience has felt the same way. Just give me a job, point me in a direction, and I'll figure it out from there. But how many times could I have avoided breaking down if I would've spent more time planning for what I'd really need for the journey ahead? Taking time in the beginning saves lives in the end.

2) If on every crazy, confusing trip you can figure out just one piece of the puzzle, you're making substantial progress.

Do you remember the clues you'd get playing Carmen Sandiego? Yeah, I don't either. I couldn't even decipher the words in the clue, let alone figure out what the clue was trying to show me. Either Carmen Sandiego was made for future Harvard grads or I wasn't the sharpest sleuth in the agency. Probably a little of column A, little of column B.

Life in our 20s can feel the exact same way, can't it? You know you're getting all kinds of clues about where you should be going, but for some reason they just don't make sense. But if we keep our eyes open. Pay attention. Keep playing the game. At some point the clues will point us where we need to go.

3) Sometimes a grueling pace WILL kill you.

In Oregon Trail you could choose the pace your wagon would go between slow, moderate, or grueling and I picked grueling every, single, time. If Martha or Frank couldn't keep up and if a few oxen had to be left behind, so be it. We were going to get to Oregon as fast as possible—dead or alive (usually it was dead).

For us today, everything is on-demand and with a press of the button we can have dinner, our favorite TV show, our next date, two books, and a lamp—all at the same time. And I think we want our "big future" to be delivered with *next-day shipping* as well. We launch into new projects, businesses, or relationships at a grueling pace and then wonder why in two months we find ourselves exhausted on the side of the trail.

4) Sometimes you just have to keep going to figure out where in the world you're headed.

Playing Carmen Sandiego was about learning how to take educated guesses. Finding that sweet spot where you were about 60–75 percent sure and just clicking "Go." There was only one guaranteed way to find Carmen Sandiego. Never stop looking.

There's not too many "sure things" in our 20s. Sometimes we just need to find our "*75 Percent Sure*" and just go for it. You can only hang out in Bamako or Budapest for so long before people start to wonder.

5) Pay the extra money and get help.

In Oregon Trail you had to cross many rivers, some five feet deep, some thirty. You could plow through it with the oxen, you could float your wagon, or you could hire a guide to get you across. But the guide was $30. Yeah, right. I'll take my chances with the 10-foot rapids.

And to my dismay, my 4th grade penny-pinching would leave my wagon sinking and send Jimmy floating away, never to be seen again.

We are such an independent, I can do it myself, *stand-back-I'm-coming-through* generation that we cross too many deep rivers without help. Pay that creative graphic designer, web programmer, marketing consultant, or sales assistant. There are so many talented people out there who will help you float across that river. Hire them. Cross safely. Your wagon, and Jimmy, will thank you.

6) Carmen Sandiego was a beautiful enigma, and while she always seemed so close, she had an amazing ability to stay just out of reach.

7) If you're going on a wild adventure there's going to be casualties. No matter how much you prepare.

We all named people in our wagon for those we had crushes on. That way when, God forbid, a rattlesnake bite turned for the worse or dysentery ran its course, we'd know who we were supposed to be with by who was left at the end of the trail.

Life in our 20s is a wild, crazy, adventure and even those people who you swore you'd be with at the end, yeah come Wyoming some of those relationships might become causalities.

67

Your Parents Are Your Always-Ally.

As kids, many of us saw our parents as completely perfect. The Mystique and Magic of Mom and Dad could do no wrong.

As teenagers, many of us saw our parents as completely imperfect. The Disappointment and Disenchantment of Dad and Mom could do nothing right.

As adults, we begin to see Mom and Dad not as perfect or imperfect, but as people—with their own dreams, fears, insecurities, flaws, and strengths. In our 20s we begin to know Mom and Dad for who they really are—one adult to another.

Yes, living at home maybe there were times when things got a tad rocky. But when you're all crammed in one boat and the waves start crashing in, things are bound to get a little tense.

Now that you're learning to sail your own ship, the last thing your parents want to see you do is drown. No matter the wars you might have waged in the past, your parents are your Always-Ally.

68

Frustration can be the best guide to leading you where you need to go.

Sure, frustration is a complete jerk. It won't sit there cross-legged, all polite and quiet-like. No, it will gnaw at your insides like a rat on a corncob.

But that's why we need it.

Don't try to ease your frustration with high doses of chocolate or wine. Don't hide from your frustration with unending seasons of your new *must-watch* show.

Sit there. Take a breath. And allow yourself to be frustrated. Then figure out what frustration is saying. Listen to its voice. It's telling you the problem and asking you to find a solution. Most inventions and innovations begin with frustration, as it forces you to find a better way if you'll let it.

Let frustration cattle prod you toward your future. Let the frustration of "*This is not where I want to be*" motivate you to keep moving forward.

Go ahead. Be frustrated. Just make sure you do something productive about it.

The best way to relieve frustration is to dive headfirst right into it.

69

If your office is permeated with a culture of complacency, especially from the top down— game over. Pack your bags. Time to leave.

Need to know if your office suffers from complacency? Pretty simple. How are new ideas received? Are they explored or instantly exploded with a shotgun of *"that's not possible."* Have you been there two years and you still can't open your mouth?

Are you allowed to tackle projects outside your "job description"?

Does your boss want to work there? Does your boss's boss want to be there?

Complacency is a disease. Extremely contagious. Easily passed from one employee to another.

I'm as serious as a funeral director after a heart attack.

Because, you starry-eyed twentysomething, coming in with new energy and ideas, will be crushed over and over by tsunami waves of complacency. Until you shut your mouth, settle in, and catch the disease yourself.

In a culture of complacency there is a sick, perverted love affair with status quo. And honestly, it's going to take a lot of hard work to change it.

70

Making and keeping friends in your 20s takes intentionality.

Now more than ever we need a little help from our friends.

So why have so many of us since college discarded them like that Christmas tree air freshener? What used to liven up our lives with *pine-needle-fresh*—now a piece of highway debris.

For many of us the transition out of college has been ten-car-pile-up scary at times. You can't see, can't steer, and have no one in the car to help grab the wheel. Because all the friends who used to be in the passenger's seat have scattered like a dandelion in a hurricane.

Where have all the friendships gone and how do we get them back?

THREE TIPS TO MAKING AND KEEPING FRIENDS POST-COLLEGE

1. Well . . . Are Friends Still Important?

That's the first question. Because honestly I think some of us have concluded that in our much-too-busy lives, friends don't even crack the *Top Ten*.

Sure we "technically" don't *need* friends just like we "technically" don't need a roof over our head. But once life starts pouring down some nasty **stuff**, it's sure nice knowing there is something there to help protect you.

Are we willing to pursue this **CrazyLittleThing called friendship**? Are relationships going to be a priority, or are we going to *Lone Ranger* this thing, the final scene of our lives just you and your horse riding into the sunset?

And while that makes for a kick-booty Hollywood ending, who's actually going to be in the audience to watch it?

2. Get Involved

We need to get involved. In something. An ultimate Frisbee team, community service, young moms' support group, polar bears club, Hipster-Training—whatever you find appealing.

Church might also be a good place to find friends. Because it's most likely embedded in their religion to love you unconditionally.

3. Pick Up the Dang Phone

Honestly, I struggle at this. I see a friend calling. I want to talk. I *need* to talk. But as I begin reaching for the "Answer" button, something takes control of my hand and turns it the other way as my phone slips sadly back into my pocket like a depressed river otter back into his burrow.

That thing that has Jedi-like control over me? **My schedule**. My to-do list. My life. My time. Mine, mine, me, me, MEE. Oh yes, the dreaded ME-MONSTER has thwarted many a good relationship and conversation.

So the next time a friend calls, pick up the phone. Slay the ME-MONSTER. Yes, there are things on your list that won't be accomplished. That's fine. Because **a conversation with a friend does more to spark your creativity and enthusiasm than five Red-Bulls.**

Bonus 4: Pride Comes Before the Friend-Fall

Or even worse, I don't pick up for a good friend because I simply don't want to talk about my life. I don't want to do the ten-minute rundown about all the obstacles and non-exciting, little tangible success details of the last month. Especially if I know the friend on the other line is experiencing more success than I. Terrible I know. **Just because I can't one-up my friend doesn't mean I should hide from them.**

WHY CAN'T WE BE FRIENDS . . .

Making and keeping friends in our 20s takes intentionality. Consider this a collective challenge for you and I both to give *friending* a chance.

71

God wants writing partners.

For years I felt like I was just an actor in my own life, hanging out in a trailer smoking a cigarette as I waited for God to write a scene worth my time.

I don't think God's looking for actors. I think He's looking for writing partners. He wants us to pull up a chair, a cup of coffee, and create *with* Him. He wants us to stay up until 3 a.m. going through the painful, laborious, exhilarating process of working with Him on our own life script.

Sure sometimes the story might take on a life of its own, but ultimately I think God wants us to ask and wrestle with the question that is the driving force behind every great story—what does this character really want? *What do I really want?*

God wants you to banter back and forth with Him, dream the next plotline—heck, even argue with Him about what should happen next because you're so passionate about the story you are writing together.

I don't think God wants us to just watch our own lives with a bag of popcorn and then complain when the story isn't turning out like we thought it should. I think God wants us to help write the dang thing.

God's waiting for us to pull up a chair next to that blank page, smile, and ask, "What are we writing next?"

72

The most dangerous phrase you can say in your 20s is "if only..."

If only I had . . .

More money.

More connections.

More charisma.

More experience.

More pull.

More sway.

A better degree.

A job I loved.

A smaller nose.

A boss who understood.

15 less pounds.

Their parents.

Their skills.

Their life.

If Only . . .

THEN I would make things happen.

THEN doors would open.

THEN I'd take risks.

THEN I'd dream dreams.

THEN I'd start really living.

THEN and only THEN.

But.

Maybe it's not the lack of money, experience, looks, or charisma that's holding us back.

Maybe the only thing keeping us from NOW instead of stuck waiting for THEN is . . .

If Only . . .

We complain that our dreams have been devoured, like a lion snuck into our house and ate them for dinner. When really our dreams are being nibbled away by a mouse that is smirking right in front of us.

Dreams aren't crushed by a lack of opportunity. Or money. Dreams are silently assassinated by distraction and wishful thinking.

Most people stop dreaming before they even give themselves the time and permission to start.

If only we'd stop with "if only."

73

The biggest risk of your 20s would be never taking any risks at all.

Your 20s are not the time to play it small.

Please dream. And take risks. Ask yourself the hard questions.

Your 20s are this crazy unique season where complete freedom meets overwhelming opportunity.

However, no matter how much freedom you have in making real, adult, risky decisions, just know that decisions like getting a face tattoo are rarely a good idea.

74

Your ability to do great things will hinge on one.single.thing— your ability, or inability, to defeat the Liar.

Whenever **you're doing something worth doing, the Liar's going to attack. Every.single.time.**

WHO'S THE LIAR?

The self-helpers might call it negative Self-Talk.

The spiritual might call him Satan.

He plays a filthy game. Because when you sit down to do your work, the Liar is going to try and stop you.

And it won't be a full frontal assault like an army storming the castle. No, it will be like Gollum from The Lord of the Rings. Sneaking up next to you, whispering in your ear a soft hiss of lies. Each lie poisoned with just enough truth that only after you take a bite do you realize it's killing you.

Even as I sit here and write this now, the Liar is whispering in my ear.

"*Who are you* to write a book?"

"Who are you to encourage people to stop me?"

"You're not as creative as _____."

"Not as funny as _____."

"Not as influential as _____ and especially not _____."

"Quit now before you embarrass yourself."

His lies unnerve me, but they have not stopped my forward movement. Because after too many years of listening to his voice, I'm better equipped now at shutting his mouth.

TWO WAYS TO SHUT THE LIAR'S MOUTH

1. Speak Directly to His Lies

Some days when the battle is fierce, I literally speak these phrases out loud.

"Liar, you have not created one single thing in your entire miserable existence. How do you have any right, authority, or credibility to tell me how to do something you are incapable of doing yourself?"

"You destroy. I'm building. You mock. I'm encouraging. You criticize. I'm creating."

Giving the Liar authority to speak truth into my life is as insane as letting a wrecking ball build my house.

2. Realize there's Beauty in the Liar's Game

Here's the interesting thing about the Liar—when he starts babbling, you know you're onto something important. When he starts talking, thank him. He just revealed to you that you're on to something huge.

Thank him, and then cut off his head. We must not let the Liar get his way like a snake suffocating its prey.

Our calling, our children, and our purpose in this world—all depend on our ability to shut the Liar's mouth.

We have been given the authority to create and the Liar can't take that away.

75

Be wary of Reality Checkers.

Reality Checkers are everywhere and they love dishing out doses of reality like they're a doctor and this is the prescription you need. You know the kind. Where you share with them your **Everest-Sized Dream** and before you can even finish they rattle off the seven reasons your dream won't work. They lather you in their own fear and insecurities, and call it sound advice.

God bless them, they're just trying to give you a dose of reality to save you the pain of making a mistake, or so they say.

Well yes, God bless them, because sometimes the only things worth pursuing are the things so far beyond what we're capable of that it's 100 percent guaranteed we'll make Hummer-sized mistakes to get there.

I'm not saying don't take advice. Sure, sometimes we need some plain good sense. Sometimes we need that wild old sage to get all sage-like on us.

But that's not Reality Checkers game. No, you'll know you've been Reality Checked when you leave the conversation feeling like you've been *slammed* against the boards by a 250-pound Russian hockey player named Pavel.

Instead of Pavel the Reality Checker, give me the person who's going to take in all the insurmountable facts of my dream and tell me, "That's awesome. Heck, I say you go for it! What do you have to lose?"

Nothing. You have nothing to lose. Reality Checkers want you to believe that your plans will fail. And you know what, they're probably right. But the point of life is NOT to not fail.

Be strategic who you tell about your Everest. If you tell everyone your big dream in order for them to affirm it, your dream will be crushed way before you reach your Everest.

Maybe you *don't* need a dose of reality. Maybe you need to take a heaping spoonful of a truer reality based on the dreams and vision inside of you. Maybe where you're headed is more important than where you're at.

Reality is what you decide reality is. If reality is a scarce, dismal place where opportunities go to die, well get ready to spend a lifetime watching sweet opportunities take their last breath.

If reality is this crazy abundant place of opportunities galore where you're walking through an exotic orchard of hybrid **Plum-Mango-Strawberry Trees** with this **Giant Juicy Fruit** just waiting to be picked (even though *in reality* such a tree doesn't exist), then by golly, you're going to be eating opportunities by the mouthful.

Maybe reality is really a choice each of us makes: which *reality* is going to be more real?

I'm taking bites from plum-mango-strawberry trees on top of Everest. I'm done getting reality checked to death.

No one knows what they're doing.

Are you freaked out that you have no idea what you're doing? Perfect! So is everyone else.

Even the so-called experts sometimes don't have a clue. Sometimes they have simply mastered the art of **Perceived Credibility**.

Sometimes making your way through adulthood will feel like going through a gigantic corn maze, in the dark, after being spun around like a kid in front of a piñata. Don't be surprised if it takes more flashlights, falls, and wrong turns than you ever planned. And the only way you end up finding your way out is to burn the whole maze down.

Don't wait to feel like you have what it takes before you try.

Don't wait for confidence before you move.

Don't wait to be cast into the lead role before you start playing the part.

Don't wait, act.

Raise your hand. Say, "sure I can do that." Then figure it out from there.

You'll be surprised how quickly the act becomes a reality.

77

The secret to finding the right person to marry? Stop looking.

I remember in my 20s being obsessed with looking for *The One*. My eyes always on high alert like I was searching for an extinct bird.

Health food stores became an excuse to find some basil, quinoa, and my soul mate. Church services were spent scanning the rows, my eyes resting on a **Possible-Possibility** as I let out a "*Praise Jesus.*"

Oh, and I had some serious run-ins with "*this-is-the-one-I-swear-it.*" You know the kind. At first, you're positive it's the genuine thing. **But just like buying that knock-off pair of sunglasses, something always breaks in about a month.**

I couldn't figure out what was wrong. Why were all the girls I dated all so insecure? Why were they so unsure of who they were and what they wanted? Why couldn't I find the right person?

I was doing my usual *lament of a single* song-and-dance with my mentor Erik, when he gave me a piece of advice that changed my whole strategy.

"Stop worrying about finding the right person. Instead, start working on becoming the right person."

Why were all the girls I dated so insecure?

Because I was so insecure.

Why were all the girls I dated so unsure of what they wanted?

Because I had no clue what I wanted.

Like attracts like. And the girls I liked were a lot like me, and what we both were like, was somewhat unlikable.

I wanted to find someone to heal from my insecurities, when I really needed to heal from my insecurities, so that I could find someone.

You can't meet someone in Hawaii when you're begrudgingly walking circles around the Los Angeles airport. You can't find someone on a trip you refuse to go on. My life was spent walking around with bags filled with rotting stuff that smelled. So I attracted travelers with the same set of luggage on the same journey. Let's just say we needed a plethora of air fresheners to make it through a date.

JOB OF INNER WORK

So for years I began to intentionally travel down the rocky, scary path that Parker Palmer calls "*inner work*." I opened up my closet doors and faced the monsters I'd been harboring for far too long.

Scary creatures called insecurity, depression, anxiety, and self-hatred.

Did these monsters tuck-tail and run the first moment I shed light on them? *Heck no.* They fought for their lives and scared me to death like good monsters do. But through prayer, mentorship, honest conversations, and a few more **RelationShipWrecks**, the monsters began to shrink as I began to grow.

Stop looking for the right person and focus on becoming the right person. Sure that doesn't mean you close your eyes while walking around the grocery store or that you'll ever be a *completely* healthy person ready for a relationship.

However, *right attracts right*. And *the* more *right* you are, *the more right* your relationship will be.

If you've ever met my wife, you know the strategy paid off for me 1,000 times over.

78

The WOMS (World Owes Me Something) will receive exactly what they deserve.

Have you ever met a WOMS? A *World Owes Me Something?*

WOMS eat entitlement for breakfast, brunch, lunch, linner, and dinner. Entitlement is a tasty, sexy, seductive trap. Like Edward chowing down on Turkish Delight from the witch in Narnia, what WOMS crave most will never be satisfied. And the Turkish *Delightelment* they thought was leading them to a palace, will take them instead to a prison.

When we live being sprinkled with **But I Deserve It**, the funny thing is, we'll get *exactly* what we deserve. But like buying a replica Van Gogh, when we think we're getting the real thing, it will end up costing us way more than it's worth.

79

Knowing your Karaoke-Compatibility should be a required premarital exercise.

Before you turn that "possibility" into something much more significant, take them to karaoke. Your **Karaoke-Compatibility will tell you a lot about your readiness for happily ever after.**

LET'S EXAMINE SOME KARAOKE PERSONALITY TYPES AND THEN HOW THEY MESH TOGETHER.

The Cat in the Bath

This is the person who will fight and claw with every ounce in them before they take a step up on that stage. You have a better chance putting an alley cat in a bathtub and coming out unscathed than dealing with the Karaoke-Cat.

The Three-Drink Minimum

They're not sniffing that stage until that third drink is at least in hand. And we're not talking ginger ales.

The Double-Down

They don't need a drink, they need a duo. Unless you're standing by their side, they're not singing.

The Show Stopper

A U2 song, then Pink, then Johnny Cash, then the Chantelles. The Show Stopper doesn't care about genre just as long as the mic is in their hands. All night long. They're putting on a show and you're just their groupie.

The All-Talk

They've been talking about karaoke for a month, bragging about that time they sang a Whitney Houston song and the Earth stopped spinning. But the moment their song is up, they are mysteriously in the bathroom yet again.

The Melancholy Molly

Surprisingly, they volunteer to be up on stage first and by themselves. A little shocked by their willingness, you snag a table and wait for the show. The music starts, he or she closes their eyes (they don't need to look at the words), and next thing you know they're singing with their whole voice, heart, and soul, "Nothing Compares 2 U" by Sinéad O'Connor. They sing the song well, *a little too well*, and at the end a few people in the crowd are dabbing their eyes with their sleeves, the once raucous room now sounding more sober than a funeral service.

The Competitor

Why did they bring a piece of paper and a pen, you ask? Oh, they're keeping score. Karaoke is not something you do; it's something you win.

The Fun at All Cost

They don't care about the lyrics or the melody, they care about making it fun. For themselves and the crowd. They dance and jump and run in place. Embarrassment is not in their vocabulary. Nor is singing on key.

The Surpriser

Soft-spoken and shy, The Surpriser quietly walks up, picks a Christina Aguilera song, and before you even realize they're on stage, they bust out the first verse that makes even the bartender stop to marvel. The Surpriser finishes and walks back to a standing ovation.

KARAOKE CLARIFYING

How Karaoke-Compatible are you? The Cat in a Bath and the Show Stopper might be a great fit for each other because one can't be dragged off the stage and one can't be dragged on. The Show Stopper and the Fun at All Cost, even though they both like being on stage, it's for very different oil-and-water reasons.

The Fun at All Cost and the Melancholy Molly might balance each other out well.

If you both have a little Double-Down, a life of fun singing together might await.

Before you say "I Do," say "Yes" to a night of karaoke. A $10 cover fee and some embarrassment belting out Bruce Springsteen might save you a lot of pain and money later.

Marriage WILL NOT fix any of your problems.

Growing up, I dreamed of one day being married. Because then I would never feel alone again. *How can you feel alone when you're having a sleepover every night?*

I dreamed of being married. Because then I would no longer feel insecure about my love handles or acne flare-ups.

I dreamed of being married. Because then I would no longer want to eye-linger on the *Sports Illustrated* swimsuit edition.

I guess I dreamed of being Peter Pan because I was going to marry Tinkerbelle. My wife would sprinkle pixie dust on me and I'd be ready to fly problem-free. Forever.

I love my wife. I love marriage. But I realized fairly quickly that marriage doesn't fix any of your problems. No, marriage actually puts a magnifying glass on how many problems *you really have*.

We grow up carrying bags with our insecurities, fears, bad relationships, problems with our parents—you name it. **Newly married and living in a small apartment is no place to store a *luggage set* full of your *baggage.*** Begin to ditch those bags now.

81

Rocking adulthood is sometimes nothing more glamorous than *Patient Every-Day-Ness.*

And to not burn out on Adult *Every-Day-Ness* you need to take some **Nothing Vacations**.

What's a Nothing Vacation? It's a vacation where you do, well, nothing. Absolutely. No sightseeing. No family. No friends. Nothing. My wife and I just agreed we're taking one. Next month. No baby. No itinerary. Just sleep. Food. Books. Sleep. Food. Rinse. Repeat.

Finding your passion is un-sexy.

We talk about finding your passion like it's dating a Swedish model or driving a German sports car. It's living this audacious, bodacious, *rocktacious* life where someone offers you coffee on Monday morning, and you give them a look and say, "*No thanks. I'm fueled by awesome.*"

What a load of elephant dung.

I prayed for years for that one great idea that would propel me into a **Life of Awesome**. But then I learned that having a great idea is the easy, exhilarating part. Like going on those first few dates with your crush—all tingle and sizzle, without any of the responsibility or commitment that comes later.

Finding your passion is un-sexy. Because do you know where you find your passion? When you receive 457 no's, yet you pick up the phone again. You find your passion when it's 4:30 a.m. and you feel like a mule sat on your head all night, but you're up and working anyway.

You find your passion scared as a cat trying to run up a highway.

Your passion is not just something you do. Your passion is something you cannot NOT do. When all dreams of bestsellers and bonuses fade away. When you know something to be so true, even when friends and family tell you to stop believing a lie. When people elude that your great idea is actually quite terrible. You find your passion when it's totally failed, yet you *refuse* to let it fail. That's passion.

The most underrated tool you have to rocking your 20s is Hope.

When I felt like my 20s were smothering my face with a pillow and I couldn't breathe, I'd break away to Griffith Park—a magical land of green, trees, and hills, encased by LA.

I'd climb high above the Hollywood sign, and there, looking across vast LA-ness, I'd audibly encourage myself (quite loudly) that I had hope. That there were bigger and better plans. That this was just a short season. I would thank God that He'd already given me a way out, even when visibly there wasn't one.

Sometimes you have to climb hills and declare the truth of your bright future instead of the reality of your lackluster present.

Sometimes you have to war for hope.

You have a purpose worth pursuing and you have to keep talking about it so you don't forget.

You know you're becoming an adult when you start putting dibs on people.

"Yeah, he's MY mechanic."

"I called MY dentist."

My chiropractor. My doctor. My personal trainer. *Yes, I'm old enough to have me one of these. Just try and stop me.*

And then when you start getting all-kinds-of-official—MY accountant. MY attorney. MY acupuncturist. MY housekeeper.

Yes, I have money. Yes, I have health insurance. Yes, I have a house.

Welcome to Adultland. I am your host.

Yeah, and if you could be a sport and take your shoes off at the door that would be great. *My* carpet guy just came. Thanks a bunch.

85

Never **LOOKING** at your budget and never **MAKING** a budget is the exact same thing.

86

If you don't define success, success will gladly define you.

Success is the most subjective word in the history of subjective words.

If you don't grab some markers and paint a picture of what it looks like. If you don't light its candle to see how it smells. If you don't look it in the eye and call it by name, then you're going to chase a figment of someone else's imagination. You can't find something when you've never actually decided what you're looking for. **If you don't define success, it will stay an unidentified flying object that you'll never take a picture of.**

87

Don't worry about marrying "The One"—focus on marrying "The Four."

Why is the search for *The One* so hard?

Is it because God gets His kicks by sending us on impossible scavenger hunts? Or is it because **The One** is a magical fairy-tale creation? Like the unicorn. Beautiful, lifts you off the ground, and most importantly, isn't real?

Yes, you will marry just one person. Unless you go Old Testament or cult style.

However, is that *one person* the *only* person?

Well . . .

I married my wife over five years ago, we now have two baby girls, and I can't imagine having married anyone else.

But was she *the only one* I could've married? If I would've taken a different job after college and met my wife at a sales seminar instead of a college admissions conference, would I have somehow been out of God's will? Doomed to a life married to "The Fifth" or "The Sixth" instead of **The One**?

I don't think so.

I don't think God operates like a cruise director and if we miss the boat it leaves without us—our future husband or wife on the arm of someone else, sipping a margarita while laughing about the last real estate deal they landed.

But whether there is such a thing as **The One** is really not that important to me. **What's important is that you make a wise decision when deciding if this is the *right one* for you.**

The decision of who you marry can be based on something substantial, like a sequoia tree, the roots deep into the ground.

Or the decision to marry can be made like buying that Snickers bar at the cash register—you're hungry and well, *why wait*?

So instead of searching for this magical creature called **The One**, I propose we should be on the hunt for **The Four**—the four different relationships that need to be intertwined within the **Right One**.

AND THE FOUR WILL BECOME ONE

Best Friend

Marrying your best friend simply means that you can do absolutely nothing with this person and have a blast. A trip to Target to buy pants can feel like going to Disneyland—well, at least on a day that Splash Mountain is closed.

If you don't enjoy going to the grocery store with this person to buy eggs or changing the clothes at the Laundromat, then you might not enjoy doing marriage. **Because marriage is built on a million more mundane moments than magical.**

I have this distinct memory when dating Naomi of being stuck in LA traffic, looking over at her and thinking, "I wouldn't want to be stuck in traffic with anyone else." It was this tiny mundane moment that turned magical. That's marriage.

However, don't try to make this best friend an exact replica of your other best friends. I made this mistake for months, wondering why Naomi didn't relate to me the same ways as Cody or Mike did. Well, the friendship is different. Your wife might not tell jokes like your college roommate did. Your husband might not talk for hours into the night like your best friend from home. That's all right. Like drinking wine or a cup of coffee, they both might taste delicious, but each will have an entirely different flavor.

Lover

Attraction is super important. And attraction is not based only on looks. Personality, faith, humor, drive, passion, looks—they all factor into attraction. However, one way or another, if this person doesn't get your motor running when they turn the key, well your car might be stuck on the side of the road at the first sign of a winter storm. *Just saying…*

Business Partner

Your marriage is a business. Anyone that tells you different is trying to sell you something for theirs. Budgets, bills, savings, earnings, investments, plans for growth, money (or lack there of) can become acid on your threads of marriage. Just like you wouldn't start a business with someone without talking through the realities of financial situations, budgets and goals, same for marriage. **Because if he's a spender and you're a saver, and you don't talk about it—then your marriage might be spent before it can be saved.**

Wartime Ally

When married life begins to feel like a war—and it will, will you war against each other or will you war together? Life can be intense—lost jobs, lost loved ones, and lost hope. So when the bullets start to fly, will you hunker down in the bunker together? Or will you be the first to turn and pull the trigger? When everything begins to war against your marriage, will the two of you fight for each other or will you fight against?

And this is where I think having similar faiths plays a huge role. Because when the enemy troops start scaling the walls of your marriage, it's important that you're both running to the same place for help.

DON'T SEARCH FOR THE UNICORN ANY LONGER

Let's stop searching for this mythical creature called The One. Instead let's focus on finding The Four, on marrying someone who will do the nitty-gritty details of life at our side—because that's marriage. That's real. And that's awesome.

REFRESH yourself before you WRECK yourself.

You've got big plans, dreams, and goals?

Awesome.

You can't squeeze water from a dry sponge.

There are no Take-Backs in grown-up relationships.

No matter the justification you deliver that verbal knock-out blow with, when your relationship is lying unconscious on the floor that *doesn't* mean you've won. No, actually quite the opposite.

Once your **Verbal-Roundhouse Punch** is thrown, *it's thrown.*

Just because you apologize and ask for it back, doesn't mean your sledgehammer hasn't already done its damage.

90

Marriage in your 20s can feel a lot like playing "House."

My wife Naomi just came in the kitchen and offered to make dinner. I raised my eyebrow, surprised, because unlike my childhood "House," usually it is *I* who is making dinner, *she* who is out there working.

"Sure I'm up for some dinner," I say, as I sit up straighter because sitting up straight is something grown-ups do.

As she commences dinner, I attend back to performing life-saving surgery on my old Nintendo. My heart aches, as my old friend is not responding to any of my treatments.

"Here's dinner," Naomi says.

Mournfully I walk back to the kitchen, a tad surprised at the rate she was able to turn the word *dinner* into actual food. And as I look to see what was concocted with such *dinner-ease*, I see a bowl of cereal. Blue, orange, green, purple rice nuggets wading in a milky pool—Fruity Pebbles, my favorite childhood cereal that's fed me with delightful fruity goodness for oh so many years is my dinner. And I couldn't be happier.

As I sit their munching excitedly, every bite reminding me of playing *House*—of life with pretend responsibilities—when my Nintendo was a spry young bachelor with his whole life in front of him, Naomi interrupts.

"Paul, we need to talk about our budget and really start finalizing some numbers."

Startled, I jump back. *Budget?* She puts Fruity Pebbles in front of me and now a conversation about the budget?! Am I the little rabbit she has lured out into the open with fruity deliciousness and has captured with the stranglehold of savings, college loans, and car payments? You can't mix a cereal that has Fred Flintstone on the box with a detailed ten-year savings plan.

As we go to bed that night, lying there side by side, I think about my poor Nintendo, about Fred Flintstone, about all the things I don't know under this new title of husband.

"Naomi," I speak up into the dark air, the absence of light making the presence of a confession much easier. "Do you feel sometimes like we're not grown-ups who are actually married, but just kids playing a game of House?"

"Yeah, I've felt like that a couple times. . ."

And as Naomi talks, I learn I'm not alone. She has her own insecurities about being a wife—whatever a wife is supposed to mean, supposed to be. She doesn't feel the part sometimes. Is she supposed to be like her mom, like my mom, like the elderly lady at church who is always offering Naomi her sage advice? She's learning about wife, just as I am husband. She doesn't have it all figured out either. And I love her dearly for it.

Naomi loves saying, "We get to create our marriage." And I think she's right. **Marriage doesn't define us, we define it.**

Lying there in bed, one thing leads to another as they say, and the conversation excitedly turns to something else entirely. And if I wasn't convinced before, it's pleasantly confirmed that *House* wasn't as accurate or all encompassing as I once thought.

91

The upside of your 20s—this is the best you'll ever look. The downside of your 20s—this is the best you'll ever look.

You spend a few good years on top and then without warning you start rolling down the other side of the hill.

Those few solo gray hairs turning into an ensemble cast.

Not only does your hair begin to recede, but to your disbelief, so do your gums. *Seriously, that's possible?*

Cracked molars, knee, back, hamstring, thyroid problems—the rubber-band-ness of your body begins to stop snapping back into place. A night on the town or two-hour football game now taking a week to recover from.

And as I watch my hair retreat like a cowardly army, I'm keeping my fingers crossed. Because going bald is like playing the lottery. You don't know if your head's a winner until you've scratched it all off.

Your 20s are about experiencing the first signs of **Retroactive Puberty**—just when you've become used to your body, it starts going through changes again.

92

"When will I feel like myself again?" The answer—never.

I spent oh so many years in my 20s feeling like I was playing a never-ending game of hide and seek with myself, and at some point I was going to jump out and yell, "Surprise, you found me!"

Then I figured out the secret—I will never feel like myself again. Because I was holding on to a Me that I could no longer be. Like that photograph Michael J. Fox holds in *Back to the Future*, **Old Me** was fading fast and not even an epic guitar solo could bring it back.

It's like our **Self-Bust** that we spent years creating has in fact **Busted** all over the ground, and instead of spending our 20s down on our knees trying to find the dusty and dirty pieces to glue back together, we should just work on building a new sculpture. And once we're done with this new masterpiece, it will be time to start another.

You will have lots of versions of yourself over your lifetime. Stop trying to download **YOU 1.5** when you need to start developing **YOU 3.3**. Let's leave the Old-Me's in the *Me Hall of Fame* where they belong and work on creating the new.

Being lost might be the exact spot that you will be found.

I, _____, am a twentysomething and I am exploring.

Or I'm lost?

I'm not sure which one.

I brought supplies. I prepared. I thought I knew the way, but I think I took a left when maybe it was supposed to be a right?

Or a left, then a right, then a left? Or right, right, left . . . *oh I dunno.*

Nothing looks familiar. The birds circling above me seem to be growing in numbers. And I'm scared, to be honest. Actually, I think FREAKED OUT would be more accurate.

I don't have a map, my mom, Pocahontas, or a furry little animal to show me the way back home.

But wait, where's home? What's home?

That's why I went exploring in the first place—to find that place where I could unpack my clothes and start my life. How can I go back to something that I set out to discover? How can I go back to something that no longer exists?

Home is the *New World*. I will find it or die trying.

Okay, not really *die trying*. That sounded dramatic, so I wrote it.

No, really, I was dying *waiting*.

I was dying when my nights were spent watching B movies to forget about my D+ life.

Sure I'm scared now. More than ever. But I'm also alive now too. I have a certain focus. A certain kind of adrenaline and drive fueling me, compelling me to keep moving forward.

Yeah, I'm lost. But that was the whole point. **Being lost might be the exact spot that I can be found.**

Explorers get lost on purpose, with purpose. Explorers only find something greater if they first lose site of the familiar.

I will not go on this journey alone. Lewis had Clark. Neil Armstrong had Buzz Aldrin. Explorers always have a party—a support group to help, to guide, and save. I'm calling in help.

Then when morning comes I'll move forward. All explorers have to get lost. That's when they make their biggest discoveries.

I, _____, am a twentysomething and I am exploring.

Truly going after your dream can feel like rappelling into the Grand Canyon—

enormous,
**overwhelming,
breathtaking,**
and a very real feeling
that you might
**fall to your
DEATH.**

95

Anyone who is selling you a formula or seven-step-process for guaranteed success in your 20s is a liar or a con artist.

(Unless it's coming from me. Then you'd be crazy not to snag it for $19.99).

Watch out that social media doesn't become death by validation.

Why was I so anxious?

It was Sunday night. I'd just spent an amazing weekend with my 15-month-old girl. And yet, as I lay down to sleep, my heart felt tangled like five strands of Christmas lights.

Then it hit me. I'd posted a picture on Facebook, Instagram, and Twitter hours earlier and before I went to bed I'd checked my phone to see the stats.

One Like. On my award-winning photo with a caption worthy of Conan O'Brien.

I was so anxious because I hadn't received enough thumbs-up to send me to bed. And at that moment I realized something: I have a serious problem.

VALIDATION ADDICT

I'm addicted: to Likes, retweets, hearts, visits to my website. Validation from the masses is my opium. Google Analytics—my high.

Tell me I'm cool. Tell me I'm funny. Please, someone "Like" me.

Sure, in the beginning a couple RTs and Likes were enough. But quickly I needed a bigger hit. My highs and lows throughout the day based on how many people have affirmed me.

And in turn when no one sees me, or when someone comments that my article (and I quote) was "The most uninspiring thing [they've] ever read," I crash. I'm strung out on the couch, my insecurities grabbing a blunt, heavy object to begin their mutiny against me.

I'm sick of running in the *Refresh 1000*—hitting the refresh button over and over just hoping for those 1,000 Likes.

Social media has become my drug. Where are all the clinics?

GROOMED FOR VALIDATION

The thing is: I've been groomed my whole life to need validation. Good grades. Gold medals. Honorable mentions even when I fell flat on my face. I've survived on morsels from parents, coaches, teachers and friends telling me "You're good enough" my whole life. Social media didn't start this validation trend. It's just reaffirmed it.

Social media is high school all over again. I'm standing in the corner at the party hoping someone cooler than me laughs at my joke. My obsessive-comparison-disorder is now at the touch of my phone.

THE SOCIAL MEDIA CURE

Curing my addiction is simple, right? Quit cold turkey. Delete Facebook. Instagram. Twitter. Toss the iPhone in the trash. Maybe move to a monastery. Pick up a broom. Take a vow of silence.

Done and done.

But is disengaging the answer? As someone who is striving to create something worth creating, inspire others with a story, and *gasp*, make a living within this online space, I'm torn.

Content is no longer king, platform is. For anyone trying to start a business, produce movies, garner a publishing contract, book speaking gigs, sell a product, make a living—how can we not focus on receiving looks from the crowd? But is it worth it?

Am I beginning to lose my sense of self outside of the online branded self I present online?

If I only create what I feel will appeal to the masses, will I be right there with the purveyors of low-budget horror films?

How dangerous is it that validation, or the lack thereof, seeps into my creativity, identity, and motivation like a radiation leak?

So yes, I can put myself out there but I can't live for the high of validation. My self-worth can't be based on how many people give me their clicks of approval.

I should feel the same after fifty thousand Likes and after one.

Easier said than done.

Will I be able to escape the clutches of validation?

I pray so.

97

You don't learn what it means to be married until you learn what it means to stay married.

You have this great big party. Delicious food. Maybe some fun dancing. Bridesmaids to the left. Groomsmen on the right. Toasts and hugs and rings and bouquets and cakes and kisses and first dances, *then poof*, it's done.

It's a day—an amazing day, the best of days, an extremely significant, life-changing, expensive day. But it is one day. Getting married doesn't happen in a day, it happens in a decade. And even that decade is merely just cutting the cake before the real party begins.

I remember going to weddings and admiring the sheer maturity and wisdom of the couple at the altar. *There's two people who have it all figured out*, I'd think.

But then you get married and realize the truth; you have marriage figured out until the day after you're actually married. We spend so much time and effort on getting married; we forget that the real point is staying married.

Learning how to make decisions together—both small and big takes practice. Because you've had just one person to plan around for years—*yourself.* Just like trying to master synchronized swimming, it takes hours of practice and near drownings before you'll even come close to swimming together.

Now as I enter **Five-Years-Deep** into the **World of Husband**, there are only two things I'm sure about:

1. I still have a lot to learn.

2. When in doubt, do the dishes.

98

A Dad's love is a TIDAL WAVE.

There is no amount of hyperbole to describe the most exhilarating, terrifyingly, momentous moment in my "Adult" life as I watched a woman I was once so nervous to kiss, now literally give her life for me, and more importantly, for six pounds fifteen ounces.

Toes, fingers, hair, hiccups, and yes even poop, all carry a weighty significance that is unlike anything I've ever experienced before. People always tell you that having a baby changes everything and you smile and say "I know" without any idea that when they say "everything", they mean, well, *everything*.

Here are just a few words I now know that I didn't know at all.

- **PRAYER**—Something so holy and pious, done in respect and esteem in church pews, became something entirely different that night. When all I could see was blood and all I could hear was "heart rate dropping" and "umbilical cord wrapped around neck," prayer became a violent shout for help—a plea of desperation and expectation, not just for God to listen, but for God to show up and save ASAP.

- **BEAUTY**—A word used for the front covers of magazines was anything but air brushed as that first sign of *baby* became my truest definition of the word. The huddled, shivering, and crying mess covered in embryonic residue made the super-model on a magazine cover look like mud splattered on a windshield.

- **SLEEP**—Something so plentiful, now a commodity rarer than finding gold in my backyard.

- **LOVE**—The word most transformed of them all. How anemic was my understanding of love just days before.

LOVE OF MY WIFE

Standing with her in what must be the most helpless position a man could ever be in, offering nothing else but my hand and reminders to breathe, the roots of my love for my wife moved deeper and further into the ground. As a young couple dating years ago, professing our love in romantic bliss, we had no idea what that word truly meant. I caught a glimpse of it that night.

And that my wife is one tough woman who is way stronger than me.

LOVE FOR THIS LITTLE GIRL

The intensity of this love became very clear to me when I found myself bawling the moment I saw her enter into the world.

Then hours later when I found myself standing over her like a grizzly bear over its cub after a nurse had the audacity to prick her with a needle and make her cry.

LOVE OF A FATHER

As I drove home from the hospital, John Mark McMillan's "How He Loves" echoed through my speakers, bringing with it another wave of tears (*geesh*, having kids makes you all soft and stuff).

My relationship with God has been up and down the last few years. Some days He feels like He's sitting close to me on the couch.

Other days He feels as warm as a frozen cod. But as I came back from the hospital, I was overwhelmed with how profound God's love must be for me.

Feeling the impact of being a father for the first time, I caught a glimpse of what our relationship has been the whole time. God's love is not mere poetry. It is a tidal wave.

99

Success in your
20s is more about
setting
the table
than
enjoying
the feast.

100

There is a lost art in America today. A forgotten custom, a lost role. We no longer desire to become the "A word"—an apprentice. You get paid peanuts, but it's worth more than anything.

There's this amazing indie-documentary that not many have seen titled *Danielson: a Family Movie (or enter a joyful noise here)*.

It's about Daniel Smith, aka Brother Danielson, and his indie-music playing, modestly successful, bizarre, brilliant, wearing nurse outfits to promote the healing of God while playing music in dive bars, family.

The documentary is about faith, doing what you love, and staying true to your creative voice. As you watch a very driven and determined Brother Danielson you can't help but wonder if he's insane or a genius, and then you land that most likely it's both.

As the documentary progresses a very nuanced storyline interweaves throughout—simple, barely visible, and yet profound.

Whenever one of the Danielson Family can't make a show, someone has to fill in and one guy in particular seems to show up more than most—a skinny, likeable, quiet, brown-haired man who, at 24 or 25 years old, takes it with a smile and laugh as Daniel's 18-year-old brother teaches him how to play a song.

This guy ends up filling in for every family member and playing almost every instrument in the band. Then as the family begins to move on and pursue their own life, and it's just Daniel playing by himself, there's the skinny brown-haired guy carrying Daniel's equipment, helping Daniel slip into his Nine-Fruit Tree costume (*yes, he wears a tree*), and then going to the back of the stage to play the banjo.

Then Brother Danielson helps this brown-haired guy produce a record called *Seven Swans*.

Then this brown-haired guy begins opening for Brother Danielson's shows.

Then this brown-haired guy produces his own record called *Illinois*.

Then this humble skinny guy named Sufjan becomes the critically acclaimed, selling out amphitheaters, hailed for creating one of the most important albums of the decade, *Sufjan Stevens*.

DON'T LEAD THE BAND

So many of us desire and dream of being front and center on stage, and we focus all our energy on getting there. When maybe a better use of our time would be to become a roadie. To be a back-up singer. To be the guy behind the guy so that you can learn everything about being the guy yourself.

Because even though we think we know how to do what we want to do—we don't.

And even though we know we're ready for the big stage front and center—we're not.

We must learn how to do as *they* do before we can do for ourselves.

You'll be much better at leading your own band if you've learned how to play all the instruments yourself.

The most
IMPORTANT
secrets are the
ones you figure
out for
YOURSELF.

The Secret to Applying the 101 Secrets

We made it! 101 Secrets. *Now what?*

Good question.

How do we take these 101 secrets and apply them to our lives in a practical, tangible way that positively and profoundly changes the course of our lives?

The creative part me of wants to say—*well*, we don't. This book is not meant to be a step-by-step plan, but a conversation starter and instigator to prompt us to think, speak, and believe differently about our lives.

Then there's the practical part of me that wants to say—here's a simple three-step action plan to take these secrets and run faster and with a clearer direction than an Olympic sprinter being chased by an angry monkey throwing unusually large mangos. And since I'm getting paid the big bucks to have all the secrets, here are three more secrets to applying all the secrets.

3-STEP NOT-SO-SECRET ACTION PLAN TO APPLYING THE 101 SECRETS

1. Twentysomething Soiree

I love the idea of 4–13 friends getting together and talking through this book.

Not only would that increase my sales, thus prompting my seven-year, get-rich-quick scheme to finally come true, but more importantly, if this book is read and absorbed alone then it kind of misses the point. Maybe I'll create some sort of *101 Secrets Experience Guide* to help prompt conversation, but I think if you just decide to intentionally meet for 6–8 weeks, you'll know what to talk about. The overwhelming theme that I hear over and over is that twentysomethings feel all alone. Be the first to reach out your hand and debunk that lie.

I definitely want to help spark this dialogue as much as possible, so I've been working diligently to create AllGroanUp.com/conversations—a place to share ideas, questions, struggles, wins, and losses with fellow like-minded twentysomethings. Check it out and see if it helps. This twentysomething shoot ain't easy! Let's talk about it.

2. Get All Visual on Your Bad Self

I don't know about you, but I need visuals of quotes and goals around my house so I can consistently remind myself of where I'm going and what is motivating me to get there. I've created some cool visual prints and posters of some of these secrets that can go up on walls and refrigerators that you can snag, but feel free to create your own as well. I would love to see what you can create from these secrets and post on your website/Instagram/Pinterest board.

Don't stash these secrets away or they will forever remain a secret. And that's just silly.

3. Think Bigger and Further Out

Yes, our plans haven't exactly gone as planned, but that doesn't mean we should think smaller. No, I think it's actually the opposite. We need to thinker bigger and way longer. Sometimes we get so immersed in the immediate that I think we lose sight of the big picture.

Right now, I want you to write down what you will be doing in 20 years. Don't just put down a title or a list of things; no I want you to tell your story in *first person present* as if you're *actually living out a day in your life 20 years from now.*

Where are you living? What time do you get up? What are you wearing? Where are you headed for work? Who are you meeting with, etc? Write down the story of your entire day. A mentor of mine, Ray Rood, had me do this and it was an unbelievably life-giving and freeing experience. It helped me unwedge my head from the dark and dismal places where it had been stuck for far too long, to take a look at the amazing view.

Now take that 20-year vision and write your story at 15 years from today. Then ten years, five years, one year, then three months from today. Then give yourself goals for what you need to accomplish in the next three months to begin walking toward your life story that you've just written.

Snag those friends you've been having a twentysomething soiree with and share your stories together. Put your goals on paper and talk about them. Your story is not a one-person show; invite some people into the audience to give you some feedback and cheer you on as you step into the part you were made to play.

THIS IS ME, SIGNING OFF

Thank you. This book would not be in your hands without your incredible generosity in sharing that first "21 Secrets for your 20s" post that changed it all. Thank you, gracias, xie xie, Mille Grazie, a thousand times over.

And can I just say, I'm really excited for you! Even if life feels like you're driving through a blizzard right now—you can't see a thing, the roads are slick, and there's a very real fear you might get stuck and not be able to get out—I promise, come morning when the sun does what it always does, the beauty around you will make the hard drive to get there so worth it.

And don't be a stranger! I know that's like writing in someone's yearbook: *Let's hang out this summer!,* but I'm serious. Here's how you find me 24/7 (well, in between a nap here and there).

AllGroanUp.com

Twitter.com/PaulAngone

Facebook.com/AllGroanUp

Pinterest.com/PaulAngone

Acknowledgments

First and foremost, thank you to my wife and best friend, Naomi Angone. Thank you for taking a last name that kind of rhymes with your first. Thank you for marrying me when I was unemployed, with college loans as the only thing to my name. For editing every line of every chapter, for making the whole book better—for making me better. For supporting my numerous crazy dreams. For never letting me give up on myself.

Thank you to my daughters Hannalise and Sierrah for being all the inspiration I could ever need to work harder, faster, and better in less amounts of time because I'd much rather be spending every minute with you.

Thank you to Ginger, Louie, and Chad Angone for being my encouragement to keep dreaming and moving forward.

Thank you to the Ramos and Wells family for your generous love and support.

Thank you Randall Payleitner, Natalie Mills, and the incredible team at Moody Publishers for your creativity, ingenuity, and courage to draw a little outside the lines with me and this book!

Thank you to my amazing community of fellow dreamers and passionate pursuers of all things awesome, for pushing me, teaching me, and supporting me in ways I will never be able to repay. Thank you Jenny Blake, Jeff Goins, Joe Bunting, Joy Eggerichs, Kevin Thomas, Micah Gallagher, Megan Atkinson, Therese Schwenkler, Allison and Darrell Vesterfelt, Justin and Trisha Zoradi, Ray Rood, Dr. David Bicker, Tanya Marcy, Matt Appling, Diana Antholis, Rob Broadus, Sam Melvin, Brent Boekestein, Jonathan and Lesley Miller, Adam York, Zack and Laura Turner, Jeff Hunt, Emily Hughes, and all my awesome coworkers at Azusa Pacific University.

Thank you to the amazing musicians who were my inspiration while I wrote. No way I could've done this without you. My book-writing playlist consisted of: Mumford and Sons, The Lumineers, Sufjan Stevens, M83, Arcade Fire, Johnny Cash, Edward Sharpe and the Magnetic Zeros, Savoir Adore, Youngblood Hawke, and Of Monsters and Men.

Then of course I have to thank you, beautiful reader you, who bought this book and is still reading this far. Without you this book would've been very lonely.

How do you pack for all fifty states?

packing light
thoughts on living life with less baggage

Allison
Vesterfelt

978-0-8024-0729-0

When I was in college, I figured my life would come together around graduation. I'd meet a guy; we'd plan a beautiful wedding and buy a nice house—not necessarily with a picket fence, but with whatever kind of fence we wanted. I might work, or I might not, but whatever we decided, I would be happy.

When I got out of college and my life didn't look like that, I floundered around, trying to figure out how to get the life I had always dreamed of. Just when I had given up all hope of finding the "life I'd always dreamed about," I decided to take a trip to all fifty states . . . because when you go on a trip, you can't take your baggage. What I found was that "packing light" wasn't as easy as I thought it was.

This is the story of that trip and learning to live life with less baggage.

also available as an ebook

MOODY
PUBLISHERS

www.MoodyPublishers.com

WHAT IT MEANS
TO BE A MAN

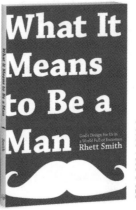

It is culturally confusing to be a man today. We are: Leaders, Videogamers, Bodybuilders, Christians, Husbands, Breadwinners, Hunters, Pushovers, Dads, and we try on all kinds of other identities. But who are we really?

By looking at history, our culture, the clichés of manhood, the Bible, and what intimacy with God looks like—this short book will offer up hope and a new perspective for men to rethink what it means to be a man in today's world.

also available as an ebook

MOODY
PUBLISHERS

www.MoodyPublishers.com

THE BIG STORY

978-0-8024-0857-0

Everybody has a story. And everybody on the planet believes some larger story in order to make sense of the smaller story of their life. We want our lives to fit within a larger plot—complete with a sense of history, conflict resolution, forward movement, and future.

So, the better question to ask is, "What sort of story are you in?"

Most people believe false stories that leave them disillusioned, enslaved, and hopeless. Secular stories of chasing success and religious stories of doing good works can both leave us feeling exhausted and empty. Only Christianity, only the old and ongoing story of the Bible, offers a story that's big enough to make sense of both the beauty and brokenness in our lives and in our world. At the center of this story is a God who disturbs our life in order to set us free.

also available as an ebook

MOODY
PUBLISHERS

www.MoodyPublishers.com